MURDER & MAYHEM IN YORK COUNTY

MURDER & MAYHEM IN YORK COUNTY

Joseph David Cress

Published by The History Press
Charleston, SC 29403
www.historypress.net

First published 2011

ISBN 978.1.60949.188.8

Cress, Joseph David.
Murder & mayhem in York County / Joseph David Cress.
p. cm.
Includes bibliographical references.
ISBN 978-1-60949-188-8
1. Murder--Pennsylvania--York County--History. 2. Violent crimes--Pennsylvania--York County--History. 3. York County (Pa.)--History. 4. York County (Pa.)--Social conditions. 5. York County (Pa.)--Biography. I. Title. II. Title: Murder and mayhem in York County.
HV6533.P4C745 2011
364.152'30974841--dc23
2011020493

CONTENTS

Contents

ACKNOWLEDGEMENTS

First, I thank my wife, Stacey, for her love, support and understanding. Because of you, I am living the dream of being an author. You truly are my inspiration.

Special thanks also go out to family and friends who have encouraged me over the years, including my father, Paul Robert Cress, and my best friend, Timothy Wolfe.

My gratitude goes out to all my past and present editors, including Hannah Cassilly of The History Press and the leadership team at the *Sentinel* newspaper. I appreciate all of the opportunities and support you have given me over the years to shape my skills to meet the challenges.

Lastly, I want to thank the professional and helpful staff at the York County Heritage Trust in York, Pennsylvania. From the start, I was impressed by the quantity and quality of material available in your research library. My appreciation also goes out to James McClure and Brad Jennings of the *York Daily Record* for their help in securing images.

INTRODUCTION

What is light without darkness? People may ask, "Why focus on crime? Isn't there something more cheerful to write about?" But where else but crime can you see the range of human weakness play out as a drama on the stage of real life? For it can be said that every murder trial is a morality play—its own separate experiment on whether the system truly works and whether justice can prevail.

It is human nature to be morbidly curious. As a journalist with twenty years of experience, I can tell you that crime reports and obituaries are consistently the most read stories in newspapers. Breaking news of murder and mayhem tends to draw the most hits on media websites. It all boils down to two basic questions: "Who do I know has died?" and "Who do I know has misbehaved?" Deep down, however, shouldn't the questions be, "What shape is the darkness taking today?" and "What kind of shadow are *we* casting on the wall for all to see?"

If you really think about it, the shadow is crime—the deepest shades of which are murder. The wall is our society, a blank page we fill every day. And the light is the law, morality, faith, love, history and journalism giving the shadow definition and boundaries. Without the light, the shadow could overcome us all. I'm not saying that we should embrace the shadow—only see it for what it is.

For seven months, I spent my free time in a dimly lit corner of my attic office writing about assorted chaos while listening to scary movie soundtracks. You hold in your hand a mixture of murder and mayhem, both high profile and virtually unknown. There are nineteen sections arranged chronologically under six themes. Within these pages are the confessions of the condemned,

York Dispatch staff, circa 1895. *From the collection of the York County Heritage Trust, York, Pennsylvania.*

the musings of poets, eyewitness testimony and media reports spanning more than two hundred years of York County history.

It has often been said that journalism is history in its first draft. It is from the pages of newspapers and the footage from a scene that we get the first inkling of a tragedy or triumph. Only later do historians and scholars take over to interpret an event and put it into context. Much of what follows is based on firsthand accounts by fellow journalists—many of whom had their names lost to history before bylines were a common newsroom practice. This book is my tribute to them and to their hard work and dedication.

Brace yourself going forward. This book is not for the meek or fainthearted. The language is gritty, graphic and straightforward to paint the truest picture in words. True crime can be an ugly, savage beast prone to fits of outrage and insanity that can grab you by the lapel and shake you out of the ordinary. But remember: the substance of every shadow is what we make of the light.

PART I
BITTER DIVIDES

The children were playing with fire—this was how one conspiracy of violence ended and another was rumored to have begun. This first theme illustrates how racial tensions had long simmered beneath the surface of York and only needed a spark to ignite the tinderbox. The "Negro Conspiracy of 1803" and its arson fires ended abruptly with a young girl's foolishness. It is widely believed that the race riots of July 1969 began after a black twelve-year-old boy, playing with lighter fluid, accidentally burned his face and blamed it on white gang members. Though he later recanted his story, the truth could not extinguish the spark. The weeklong riots killed two people, injured thirty others and caused property damage estimated at $150,000 in today's money. The violence was so intense the National Guard had to be called in the morning of July 22 and Governor Raymond Shafer had to declare a state of emergency for York. The Negro Conspiracy and York race riots represented, respectively, the earliest and most recent cases of true crime profiled in this book.

"One Common Ruin": The Negro Conspiracy of 1803

It was beyond anything ever seen before in York Borough. Five wooden barns full of hay and straw were on fire all at once, creating a massive blaze that threatened the whole town. The mystery villains had struck again, and the constant fear and need for vigilance was taking its toll on borough residents.

Disheartened, they must have wondered when it would stop and if anyone would die in the process. It was March 14, 1803.

This latest disaster began at 5:00 p.m. when flames suddenly burst out of a barn owned by Mr. Zinn. Within minutes, the fire had spread to four adjacent barns before combining into an inferno. The situation looked grim but for a welcome change of fortune as reported in the *York Recorder*:

> *With great exertions and a providential change of wind, the houses and other buildings near this scene of desolation were saved. The inhabitants are worn out with watching...and sickening under the apprehension of greater calamities.*

Borough residents could not have known that this was the last in a string of fires to plague York in a three-week period spanning February and March 1803. They would learn later that this rash of arson was the work of several

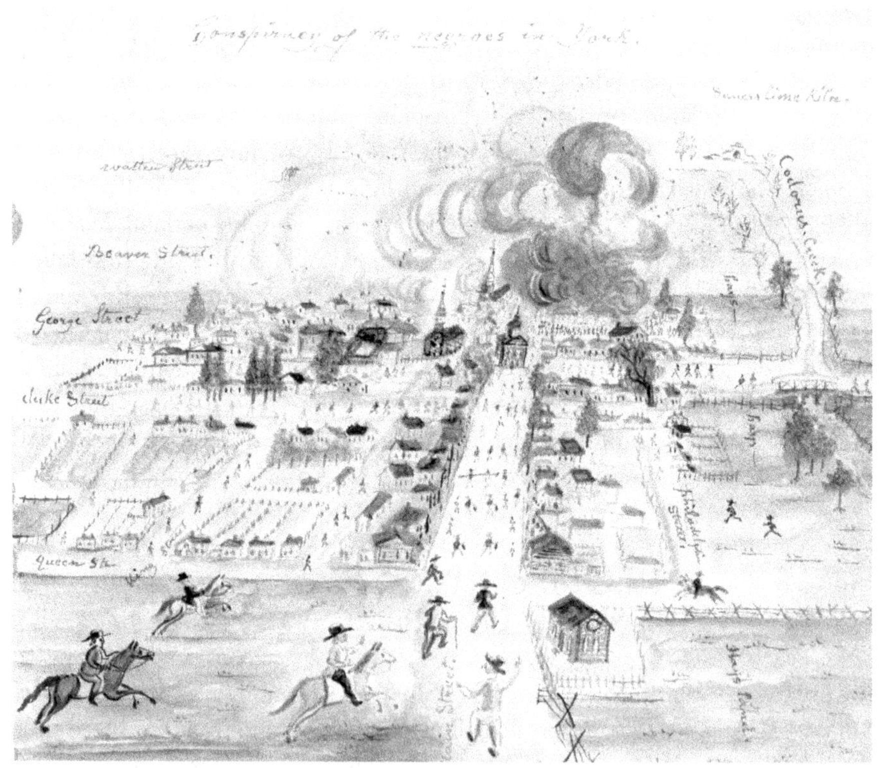

A sketch done of the Negro Conspiracy of 1803 by folk artist Lewis Miller. *From the collection of the York County Heritage Trust, York, Pennsylvania.*

blacks disgruntled by the recent conviction of Margaret Bradley, a black woman sentenced to four years in state prison on charges that she tried to poison two York women. This conspiracy operated so efficiently at first that no suspicions fell on black citizens.

The first fire was reported in a stable at about 4:00 p.m. on February 20. The conspirators chose their target well—this building shared a roof with a kitchen and stood within a few feet of a stable on an adjoining lot that had a large quantity of hay. By the time it was discovered, the fire had spread so rapidly that there was no way to save the first stable.

Instead, local residents focused on saving the surrounding buildings. They were helped by calm winds and roofs made damp by the winter frost. Responding fire engines were aided at the scene by the "spirited and well directed exertions of some young men, who tore the roof off the kitchen," the newspaper reported.

The second fire was discovered at about 8:00 p.m. on March 7 between the stables of two local doctors. Before any resistance could be mounted, both buildings were enveloped in flames, and the fire spread rapidly to a third stable. A reporter with the *York Recorder* described the scene that followed: "Three buildings were all on fire…and sank down in one common ruin. By uniting and mingling their flames, they formed a most tremendous fire, which threatened a great part of the town…The exertion of citizens…under favor of a calm night, succeeded in confining the devouring element."

The fires showed that there was a need for increased vigilance through foot patrols. The arsons also demonstrated the value of constantly keeping apparatus in good repair, fire companies organized and leaders in place to issue orders during emergencies. The *York Recorder* criticized the local fire companies for not doing enough to maintain readiness:

> [They] *have been applied to again and again during the winter to make preparations against accidental fires…They have been constantly admonished by the calamities which have almost generally befallen the neighboring towns, but all to no purpose. They sat with their arms folded until the cry of the fire startled them into activity—then no ladders nor hooks were to be found—no engines in order—and it more owing to Providence, and the exertions of the citizens, the town has been preserved from total destruction.*

In particular, the newspaper acknowledged the efforts of local women in helping to put out the fires: "The Fair Sex deserves the highest praise…They are patterns of exertion, presence of mind, and patience under fatigue, even to the men." The *York Recorder* even offered advice to women, suggesting that they hand over wet blankets to the men so they can spread the damp fabric over neighboring roofs to contain the fires. The newspaper also suggested women staff the empty bucket side of the bucket brigade so that "their exertions may be longer continued" and they can avoid being splashed.

Fear had reached such a fever pitch that Governor Thomas McKean issued a March 17 proclamation offering a $300 reward for any information leading to the arrest and conviction of the arsonists. McKean also promised to pardon any conspirators who came forward with full disclosure on the origins and activities of the group, including the names and addresses of those involved. He ordered law enforcement countywide to be extra vigilant in tracking down "a most wicked and daring conspiracy…formed for the purpose of burning the borough."

Local authorities published a notice on March 21 advising residents of the borough and the countryside to keep their "negroes and people of color" at home under strict discipline and not allow them to come into York for any reason without a written pass from the justice of the peace. The notice warned slave owners their property needs to leave town at least an hour before sundown "on pain of being imprisoned or at risk of their lives."

The conspiracy was betrayed by the poor judgment of a black girl who had received instructions to set fire to Mr. Zinn's barn at twelve o'clock. The girl was arrested after she mistook midday for midnight and openly carried a pan of coals into the barn at noon to scatter on the hay. She confessed, giving authorities the information they needed to arrest other conspirators the following week.

Twenty-one blacks and mulattoes were charged with arson and brought to trial in May. Of the defendants, four plead guilty and four plead not guilty. Two who plead not guilty were later convicted by a jury. Five were sentenced to twelve years hard labor in prison, with six of those years in solitary confinement. A sixth conspirator received five years hard labor in prison, including six months of solitary confinement. The newspaper named none of the accused, and there was no specific mention of the girl's fate.

During sentencing, the court scolded the conspirators for their ingratitude by reminding how the efforts of state lawmakers to free blacks from slavery had resulted in some blacks obtaining the rights of free men. Blacks who were suspects in the conspiracy but cleared of indictments by the grand jury were ordered by the court to post bail for their release on good behavior.

The same news story that announced the fate of the conspirators made a possible reference to the Underground Railroad in stating that York Borough was "infested with disorderly houses" that serve as rendezvous points for blacks. The story praised the efforts of a local leader to censure those magistrates and burgesses who allow such houses to be kept in town: "We have often with grief viewed the apathy of our magistrates with regard to the suppression of vice and immorality, but...hope they will...act more consistent with their oaths of office."

The story also fixed partial blame for the conspiracy on the abolition society in York, as seen in these excerpts:

> *Their conduct...is, in our opinion, inimical to the peace and happiness of the town. We do not call in question the purity of the motives that give rise to this society. Like other good intentions, they are liable to be abused...The consequence of which...has afforded an asylum for many...fugitives from a neighboring state.*

"Black...White—Even": The Riot Murders

They gathered around the large candle—two families united by tragedy, trying to bridge a once bitter divide. In each hand was a small candle; the flame representing the light of a memory they cherished of their lost love. For Sharon Schaad Howe, it was of her father kissing her goodbye as she poked the top of her head out from behind the shower curtain. She was only five years old on July 18, 1969, when Henry Schaad, a rookie police officer, was mortally wounded during the York race riots. The hurried kiss on his way out the door was an image she kept fixed in her mind because there were so few photographs of her father, the shutterbug of the family.

Then there was the Allen family, with their thoughts of a mother and a sister who had a delightful singing voice. Lillie Belle had a dream of moving her children to Brooklyn and away from the racism of the segregated South. A preacher's daughter, she had faith in the future for her son, Michael, and daughter, Debra. But her dream became a nightmare the evening of July 21, 1969, when the bigotry she tried to escape took her life.

Together as one, the two families lit the large unity candle and paused in a moment of prayer. It was February 2, 2002, and they were invited by organizers to the annual African/African American Love Feast. As when they first met privately in December, the families shared smiles and fond memories of Henry and Lillie Belle. When the time came for them to depart, they hugged and said their goodbyes. A long ordeal awaited both families, who embodied a lesson that many of us, sadly, have yet to learn. Skin color doesn't matter. Blood is red all the same. Black or white, it flows the same color—no matter what.

For thirty years, no arrests were made in the 1969 murders of Henry Schaad and Lillie Belle Allen. Investigators had suspects but never enough evidence to file charges. Whether black or white, witnesses insisted that they had no knowledge of either case, but it was thought that they were trying to stonewall the investigations out of loyalty to race and family, fear of repercussions or vows to take their secrets to the grave. For decades, blacks in York city felt so victimized by the mostly white police force that many had no incentive to help investigators. Black militant groups circulated fliers: "When you are questioned about the brothers and sisters in your community, you don't know anything." Similar attitudes existed in white neighborhoods. "Everyone knew who was involved, but everyone thought it was even," former mayor Charles Robertson told *Time* magazine after his arrest in the Allen case. "One black had been killed and one white—even."

This editorial cartoon by Walt Partymiller was published in the July 31, 1969 edition of the *York Gazette and Daily*, shortly after the race riots. *Reprinted by permission of the* York Daily Record/York Sunday News.

The stalled investigation was especially hard on Russell Schaad, who remembered how his son Henry had followed in his footsteps and was sworn in as a police officer in September 1968. Until his death in 1977, the veteran detective pushed for a solution to Henry's murder. Whenever police confiscated guns or investigated a shooting, he would ask fellow officers to test the firearms for a possible match to the suspected murder weapon: a military surplus Krag infantry rifle similar to that used by American soldiers during the Spanish-American War. "Knowing he just couldn't get that little piece of evidence…just hurt him so much," Barry Schaad said of his father during a 2002 interview. Lillie Belle Allen had died the night she was shot, but Barry's brother survived for two weeks on a respirator before dying on August 1, 1969.

Public interest in both cases waned until 1999, when the *York Dispatch/York Sunday News* published a thirty-year retrospective on the riots. Fresh leads generated by the coverage prompted authorities to reopen the investigations. In September 2000, District Attorney Stan Rebert convened a grand jury, which heard testimony from more than one hundred witnesses. In the spring of 2001, the panel issued indictments charging ten men with murder in connection with the Allen slaying. Then, in October 2001, the grand jury indicted two men they believed were responsible for mortally wounding Henry Schaad.

The Allen murder trial took place in October 2002, followed in March 2003 by the Schaad trial. The following sections will go in reverse order in keeping with the sequence of when the victims were shot—starting with Schaad and ending with Allen. The trials were mirror opposites in the way lawyers portrayed the York city police force. In the Allen case, officers were cast as racist brutes who had incited the white defendants to violence against blacks. In the Schaad case, police were the victims of an ambush staged by militant blacks who gunned down a civilian.

By all accounts, Henry Schaad and Lillie Belle Allen were innocent victims caught up in the crossfire of a race war on the streets. Neither victim directly participated in the violence, nor was there evidence to suggest that either one was a racist. In both cases, a vehicle played a critical role as an important symbol of either the hatred or paranoia of the time. At the time of the shooting, Schaad was a passenger in "Big Al," a secondhand armored car donated to the city by a bank. As for Allen, the night she was killed, she was a passenger in a white Cadillac. Neither vehicle was available for examination by either the prosecution or defense. "Big Al" went missing, and the Cadillac ended up junked. No murder weapons were ever found or directly linked to any defendant. Both victims underwent two autopsies—one in 1969 and one

State police arrive at York City Hall on Saturday, July 19, 1969, during the race riots. *From the collection of the York County Heritage Trust, York, Pennsylvania.*

in 2001. Of the two trials, the Allen case drew the most attention from the national media and has been compared to the "Hex Murder" in its level of sensation. This was probably due to the fact that a former York city mayor was among the defendants.

"WE ALL DID": THE SCHAAD CASE

The riot was already underway when Henry Schaad reported for duty on July 18, 1969. He was one of three officers assigned that night to patrol in "Big Al" after the armored car was taken out of storage to provide police better protection. Prosecutors trying Stephen Freeland and Leon Wright for his murder traced the circumstances back to a July 17 shooting along West Pershing Avenue. White gang member Robert Messersmith, leader of the Newberry Street Boys, shot Taka Nil Sweeney and another black teenager while they were talking to a plainclothes police detective. Sweeney was seriously injured and had to be hospitalized for days.

The rumor spread rapidly through the black community that the shooter was a white police officer. While later proven false, it was too late to matter. Blacks had filed numerous complaints of police brutality and intimidation over the years, without any results from city administrators. So black youth rose up and decided that it was time to act. Within hours, they were attacking any white person who ventured into their neighborhood. Much of the violence was concentrated at or near South Penn Street and West College Avenue. Retired police officer Jim Brown testified that he drove through that intersection in a marked cruiser just after 10:00 p.m. on July 18. He heard gunfire from automatic weapons, along with the impact of five to six bullets hitting the car. Unhurt, Brown warned Schaad to stay away from that intersection, as the twenty-two-year-old rookie cop was preparing to board "Big Al." The circumstances were such that his words went unheeded.

Stan Gilbert was riding his motorcycle east on West College Avenue on his way home from work. He had just stopped at a red light at South Penn Street in front of Sam's Café when he saw a gun and heard a shot being fired into the air. Fearing the worst, Gilbert ran the red light, keeping as low as possible to the motorcycle frame. He had managed to travel several hundred yards before feeling the impact of a bullet that passed completely through him. Suddenly his shirt felt warm and wet. Determined to make it home, he crossed the bridge but collapsed at Oak Lane, unable to continue.

Just after 11:00 p.m., "Big Al" was in the 300 block of West Hope Avenue providing protection to firefighters working a mattress fire. Black youth were not only targeting police officers but other first responders as well. One tactic was to create an emergency and then ambush those dispatched to help. A call came in for "Big Al" and its crew to assist a motorcyclist shot on College Avenue. Officer Sherman Warner drove the car west on West Hope Avenue before turning south on Penn Street. He then turned left on West College Avenue, passing a crowd of black youth that had gathered at the intersection.

As "Big Al" moved toward Gilbert, several gunmen came out from hiding behind Sam's Café and fired on the armored car. A bullet shot from about 350 yards away struck the rear armor of the vehicle just as it was beginning to cross the bridge over Codorus Creek. The bullet shattered into fragments that pierced Schaad in both legs and on his left side below the armpit. One fragment cut a path through both lungs and injured his spine. Officer Ron McCoy was sitting beside the rookie cop when he heard a loud booming sound just before Schaad cried out, "I'm shot!" and slumped forward. As McCoy helped the injured officer to the floor and checked vital signs, Warner

Officer Henry Schaad. *Courtesy of the* York Daily Record/York Sunday News.

got on the radio and drove "Big Al" to York Hospital, where Schaad was admitted to intensive care. "We went out in the armored vehicle," McCoy told jurors. "We thought we were safe." None of the officers was wearing bullet-proof vests.

The prosecution accused Stephen Freeland of firing the fatal shot with his Krag rifle. However, ballistic tests concluded that the fragments recovered from Schaad could have been fired from any number of weapons. Commonwealth witnesses testified that Freeland had showed off his distinctive rifle and had even bragged about using it on "Big Al." Wright was also seen firing a gun at the armored car and then bragging about hitting it. Under the theory of accomplice liability, it really didn't matter who fired the fatal shot. Both men could be held equally guilty under the law.

Defense attorneys argued that prosecution witnesses were confusing the shooting of Schaad with other violent episodes at that same intersection during the riots. They also claimed that black youth fired at "Big Al" in self-defense after police allegedly paraded the vehicle up and down the streets so that officers could shout racial slurs from inside and fire their rifles indiscriminately from gun ports in the armored car. "There were a lot of people in York…that had…motive and opportunity to take pot shots at Big Al, the symbol of brutality and oppression by the York police department," said Terrence McGowan, Freeland's attorney. But Chief Deputy Prosecutor Bill Graff questioned whether it could be self-defense when "Big Al" was struck from behind while moving away from the crowd. Officer McCoy testified that no one inside the vehicle had shouted insults or fired rifles out of gun ports. The windows in the armored car could not go down, and "Big Al" was not equipped with a public address system. The officers inside only had revolvers.

Defense attorneys attacked the credibility of prosecution witnesses—many of whom had histories of crime and substance abuse. Several offered conflicting testimonies or were reluctant to even take the stand. Quite often, Graff had to hand these witnesses transcripts of their prior grand jury testimony just to refresh their fuzzy recall. Despite all of this, Graff was confident that jurors could sort through the confusion and consider the evidence, not the source. "Just because they have a criminal history doesn't mean they are lying," Graff said of his witnesses.

The most surprising witness was Michael Wright, brother of defendant Leon Wright, who was only supposed to confirm that Freeland was among the men who fired on the armored car. Instead, Michael Wright confessed on the stand by saying, "We all did," implicating not only Freeland but himself and his brother, too. This shocked everyone in the courtroom because Michael Wright had made six prior statements under oath without ever divulging his role. When asked, he confirmed that his confession was made without any promise of a reduced sentence or immunity from prosecution. His only words of explanation were, "See, you have a jury here today. This decides." Michael Wright testified how blacks had been fed up with police brutality. "Everyone was getting mad and said they were going to fight back," he explained. So they devised a plan to stop the armored car that they claim was a menace to the neighborhood.

Against his attorney's advice, Freeland took the stand and denied any involvement in the plot. Freeland testified that he and others in the black community were being targeted by a racist police department. He felt that the segregation in York was on par with the southern states. "We're talking about an era when this…country was up in race riots," Freeland told jurors. "You had a lot of heat and tension…built up from one year to the next.

National Guardsmen in armored personnel carriers patrol York streets during the 1969 race riot. *From the collection of the York County Heritage Trust, York, Pennsylvania.*

Blacks were being brutalized on a regular basis." Nevertheless, the jury found Freeland and Leon Wright guilty of second-degree murder. Freeland was sentenced to nine to nineteen years, while Leon Wright was sentenced to four and a half to ten years. Both men died of natural causes while serving time in state prison in the fall of 2005. Freeland was fifty-three years old, while Leon Wright was fifty-seven.

As for Michael Wright, he fled York city soon after his testimony but was arrested in New Orleans in January 2005 and extradited back to Pennsylvania on fugitive murder charges. He later pled guilty to conspiracy and was sentenced to eighty-six days of time served. The Schaad family objected, saying that the sentence was too light for the severity of the crime. But President Judge John Chronister told them that the sentence was in keeping with what codefendants in the Allen case had received for their cooperation. "He [Michael Wright] was the only one who spoke up and told the truth," Chronister said. The badly burned body of Michael Wright was pulled from an apartment fire in Baltimore on November 18, 2005. The fifty-five-year-old man had died of multiple gunshot wounds.

"Just Hold On": The Allen Case

In a grim foreshadowing of violence yet to come, Alexis Joy Key barely survived an encounter with a white mob on North Newberry Street. It was the early evening of July 20, 1969—the day before Lillie Belle Allen was shot. Key was a passenger in a southbound car approaching the 200 block when she noticed people in the streets and hanging out the windows. She could hear snickers before someone shouted, "N-----! Shoot the n-----!" and the gunfire began. Bullets came from every direction hitting the rear, top and front of the car. Two went through the driver's side door. Key's niece was struck near one of her eyes by either debris or a stray pellet. "We panicked," Key would testify during the Allen murder trial. "We were scared. We zoomed off that street, went through the red light and straight to the police station." But the officer there was less than sympathetic. He more or less implied that it was their fault for driving through a white neighborhood in the middle of a race riot.

There was testimony during the 2002 trial that suggested a direct link between the Schaad and Allen homicide cases. This connection first became apparent early on July 20 when the Newberry Street Boys held a meeting in Farquhar Park. Members of the white gang typically met there on Sundays to collect dues and elect new members. But this Sunday was different—the agenda focused on the riots. This meeting attracted white gangs from throughout the city and suburbs until a crowd of just over one hundred young adults and teenagers had gathered in the park.

Witnesses testified how this only became a "white power" rally after city police arrived on the scene in squad cars and armored vehicles, including "Big Al." NSB member Theodore Halloran said that these officers included Charles Robertson, who led the crowd in cheers of "white power" while pumping his fist in the air. Halloran also testified that Robertson invited gang members to look inside "Big Al" and see for themselves traces of Schaad's blood in its interior. "I was curious," Halloran testified. "I wanted to see the bullet hole that shot a police officer. I actually put my hand on top of it [the blood] to see if it was still wet. It was dry." Halloran was convinced that Robertson was angry and seeking revenge for the shooting of the white police officer.

Robertson stood out among the three white men on trial for Allen's death. By 2002, he had served two terms as city mayor but had to relinquish his reelection bid in light of his arrest. The prosecution had accused Robertson of passing out ammunition to white gang members and then inciting them

This photograph by William Schintz of York shows the interior of the armored car in which Officer Henry Schaad was shot on July 18, 1969. *Courtesy of the* York Daily Record/York Sunday News.

to violence by encouraging them to fight off a feared invasion of their neighborhood by black militants.

Attorneys representing Robert Messersmith and Gregory Neff—the two other defendants on trial—argued that the shooting of Allen was a tragic accident caused by white gang members who acted in self-defense after the police played on their fear. It came out at trial that police officers had told stories that the Black Panthers were on their way to Newberry Street to confront the white gangs. There were reports that the Federal Bureau of Investigation (FBI) was monitoring the black militant group and that a reliable source said that forty Black Panther members were heading for York.

Two other incidents on July 20 support the defense's theory that a white or light-colored Cadillac had become a symbol of fear for white gang members. Arthur Messersmith, the defendant's brother, testified that he was standing on the corner of Newberry Street and Cottage Hill Road at about 9:00 p.m. when a white car drove into the neighborhood. As the vehicle crossed the railroad tracks in front of him, Arthur saw a black gunman pop out of the trunk and begin to fire on people in the neighborhood. Residents returned fire as the car drove away.

That same evening, Arthur Messersmith firebombed the Cottage Hill Road home of Frank and Marie Myers, the only black family living in the neighborhood. He testified at trial that he was drunk and probably under the influence of LSD and other drugs when he threw the Molotov cocktail at the house and fired a shot at a window awning. A neighbor extinguished the fire with a garden hose. Marie Myers had to be hospitalized after she cut herself crawling through broken glass to reach a phone to summon police.

After the firebombing, brothers James and Sherman Spells, two black men, were seen driving into the white neighborhood in a light-colored Cadillac. Arthur testified that they were there to warn his brother, Robert, that they would personally hold him responsible for any further attacks against their mother, Marie Myers. "I told him my mother had absolutely nothing to do with the turmoil," James Spells told jurors. The defense argued that the gang members may have mistaken the white Cadillac driven by Hattie Dickson—Allen's sister—for the vehicle driven by Spells.

There was testimony that the Allen shooting could have been avoided had police acted differently the evening of July 21. Vietnam War veteran Robert Stoner was employed as an outreach worker tasked with helping police monitor potential trouble spots. Stoner noticed that a large group of armed men had gathered after dark on North Newberry Street. He reported this to police captain Charles McCaffrey at least twice in the hours leading up to the shooting but was told that police were already aware of the situation. Stoner would later witness the murder.

That day, twenty-seven-year-old Lillie Belle Allen of Aiken, South Carolina, was visiting York with her parents and two children. They were there to spend time with Hattie Dickson and her husband, Murray. While the adults spent the day fishing, eleven-year-old Debra and nine-year-old Michael stayed at their aunt's home. The adults returned briefly before heading out again, this time on a trip to buy groceries. Lillie Belle assured her son Michael that she would return, but Debra Taylor would later testify to hearing something like firecrackers going off in the distance the night her mother was killed.

As Hattie Dickson drove the Cadillac toward West Philadelphia and North Newberry Streets, she noticed a yellow barricade horse standing on the sidewalk next to two police officers, who were laughing and talking to each other. Neither officer made any attempt to stop and talk to her. Thirty-three years later, police officer Ronald Zeager testified that his job the night of July 21 was to man the barricade at that intersection. He told jurors that he advised the family to use an alternate route to get to the

Lillie Belle Allen. *Courtesy of the* York Daily Record/ York Sunday News.

store and even offered directions but ended up moving the barricade and allowing them through.

In his closing statement, Henry Ness, attorney for Neff, criticized Zeager and the other officers, saying, "It's crystal clear if they had done their job, nobody would be here today." But Clyde Bennett, a Philadelphia Street resident, testified that at least one officer hollered at the Cadillac to stop before it went over the railroad tracks that bisect the 100 block of North Newberry Street. Dickson saw a gunman in a second-story window when her headlights bounced over the tracks. This caused her to panic and try to turn the car around, but it got caught up in the tracks and stalled. Meanwhile, Stoner took cover after he heard someone shout, "Here comes the black sons of bitches!" followed by the sound of gunfire for about thirty seconds. Peering out, Stoner saw a haze of gun smoke along with a body lying beside the Cadillac. A reporter captured this dramatic testimony as Dickson described the shooting to jurors: "I tried to turn the car around to go back the way we came in. They started firing. It was so many. It was so much of it. The car was rocking. Lillie Belle got out of the car. They started firing again. I heard my sister cry out to us, 'Somebody help me.' I said, 'Just hold on.'"

During a lull in the firing, Hattie Dickson thought of exiting the car to escape west on the railroad tracks, but she was stopped by her husband Murray. "They reloaded and kept on shooting," she told jurors. "We were there for a long time." Philip Grosklos saw the Cadillac bearing the family approach and heard somebody yell, "They got a gun," before the crowd opened fire. Grosklos urged the family to hunker down after he saw the terrified face of Allen's father, Reverend James Mosley, looking out the back window. He described what happened next: "A woman got out of the back and got up and looked over the top of the car. She put her hands on the roof. Within a second, there was a gunshot. It came down Newberry Street and hit her. She went down."

Meanwhile, Dennis McMaster was one of four officers manning "Big Al" as the armored car was parked about two blocks away. They heard gunfire and went to investigate. As Robertson drove the vehicle to the scene, McMaster peered out of the front windshield and rear gun ports. He saw people armed with rifles and shotguns on the porches and in the windows and doorways. A woman's body was lying on the ground next to a shot-up Cadillac.

"I went over to the car," McMaster told jurors. "I was just amazed. There were three to four people lying on the floor of the car. I asked, 'Is anybody hurt?'" Lillie Belle was the only family member hit during the gunfire. She later died at the hospital. McMaster advised Dickson to drive back the way they came. He radioed police but got no response from officers tasked with manning the intersection of North Newberry and West Philadelphia Streets.

A short time later, Debra Taylor heard a scary *bloop* sound approaching her aunt's home. "It started off low but got louder," she told jurors. It turned out to be the sound of a Cadillac riding on its rims after its tires had been shot out. Her brother, Michael Allen, testified that he saw his grandparents enter the house with sad looks on their faces. When Michael asked about his mother, they just looked at him blankly. The night passed with a lot of crying from the adults. He woke the next morning and saw the damage. That's when his grandmother Beatrice Mosley told him what had happened.

From the start, the commonwealth accused Robert Messersmith of being the man who fired a shotgun shell that struck Allen in the chest. In his closing statement, prosecutor Tom Kelley reminded jurors how witnesses identified Messersmith as the gunman who stood in the middle of the street in a posture of offense, not defense. Kelley argued that both Messersmith

Rear view of the Cadillac that Lillie Belle Allen was riding in when she was shot on July 21, 1969. *Courtesy of the* York Daily Record/York Sunday News.

and Neff had a legal duty to first retreat to their homes before using deadly force to defend themselves. "There is no such thing as a right to protect a neighborhood," Kelley said.

Some of the most damaging testimony against Messersmith came from former NSB member Charles Fidler, whose apartment became the party house of the gang during the late summer of 1969. That August, gang members bragged about killing Allen, saying, "We got her." At that point, Robert Messersmith stood up and punched a hole in the wall, declaring that he alone had shot the black woman. Defense attorneys attacked Fidler's credibility, claiming that he fabricated the story to get a better plea bargain for pending charges that included felony theft, forgery and passing bad checks.

Lawyers for Robert argued that there were too many shooters and too little physical evidence to determine who fired the fatal shot. "Bobby Messersmith is a sacrificial lamb to political correctness," said Peter Solymos. Nevertheless, the jury convicted Messersmith of second-degree murder. Two months later, in December 2002, Robert Messersmith was sentenced to nine to nineteen years in state prison. At that hearing, he identified his one-time friend Donnie Altland as Allen's killer. Investigators had already considered Altland a suspect but never had enough evidence to charge him. Altland had committed suicide the day after he was interviewed by detectives following the commonwealth's decision to reopen the case. He left behind a taped confession along with the words "Forgive me God" scrawled on a cocktail napkin.

As for Gregory Neff, the prosecution read into the record his grand jury testimony in which Neff admitted to firing three shots at the Cadillac—but only after Allen had already been shot. Neff had lost a plea bargain with the district attorney's office after he insisted that the victim had a gun in her hand and was pointing it down the street. Ness questioned how his client could be charged with murder after the victim had already fallen from her fatal wound. Neff was convicted of second-degree murder and later sentenced to four and a half to twelve years in prison.

Five other men, initially charged with murder, pled guilty to the lesser offense of conspiracy to commit an unlawful act in exchange for their testimony against Robertson, Neff and Robert Messersmith. Teenagers at the time of the riots, they were all accused of firing at the white Cadillac that had carried Allen. Rick Lynn Knouse, William Ritter, Thomas Smith, Chauncey Gladfelter and Clarence Lutzinger received sentences of less than two years in county prison. In exchange for his testimony, Arthur Messersmith pled guilty to conspiracy to commit murder and criminal attempt to kill and was sentenced to eighteen to thirty-six months in state prison.

A tenth man, Ezra Slick, pleaded no contest in May 2003 to criminal attempt to kill and conspiracy to commit an unlawful act. Slick did not rebut eyewitness accounts that he was among those who fired at the car but claimed that he had been drinking and couldn't recall his actions. Slick was serving a two- to five-year sentence in state prison when he died of lung cancer in December 2005.

A former Girarders gang member, Knouse testified that he had used ammunition provided by Robertson to fire on the vehicle. Knouse told jurors that the former police officer and city mayor encouraged him to kill as many blacks as possible. Prosecutors charged Robertson as an accessory to murder before the fact because of the allegations that he incited white gangs to violence. William Costopoulos, attorney for Robertson, argued that his client should not have been charged with homicide in the first place. Robertson was not present at the time of the shooting nor did he fire a gun at the car. The same jury that convicted Messersmith and Neff found Robertson not guilty.

In January 2003, Allen family attorneys filed a federal lawsuit against York, claiming that the city allowed police to practically deputize the white racist gangs. The lawsuit also named five police officers, four of whom—Robertson, McMaster, James Vangreen and Ray Markel—had responded to the Allen crime scene in "Big Al." The suit claimed that none of the officers made arrests, questioned witnesses or confiscated weapons at the scene. The same suit accused officer Zeager of removing the barricade that allowed the family to drive into an ambush.

While testifying during the Allen murder trial, McMaster admitted that officers failed to follow proper procedures for a crime scene. "We were frightened," McMaster said. "We were not comfortable." He was referring to the large crowd that had gathered at North Newberry Street. In addition, the crew of "Big Al" was only on the scene a few minutes before receiving a report of fellow police officers being pinned down by gunfire near the intersection of Maple and Duke Streets.

Following negotiations, the City of York ultimately agreed to pay Allen family members $2 million over ten years in exchange for them dropping the lawsuit alleging wrongful death and civil rights violations. Later, York took on $1.3 million in debt to finance a lump sum payment to the family rather than pay the damages in annual installments. The lump sum payment was made at the request of Allen family members.

PART II
FISTFIGHTS AND FIREWATER

First, pour the alcohol in a dirty shot glass. Then add some chaos, mixed in with greed. Stir in that foolish and reckless bravado. Then chill over crushed and torn-apart dreams. No matter the taste, murder can make the perfect cocktail to quench almost every bloodthirsty impulse. On tap today are two young men hung over by gory details, as well as two crowds drunk on very different blends of mob mentality. You will read about the mother who witnessed a crime in her sleep and the prizefighter who cried like a baby on the witness stand. You will hear words of outrage spoken after a rowdy invasion and see what lengths fear can drive the most sober of occasions to sudden, violent tragedy.

"Theater of Their Unblushing Defiance": The Goldsboro Prizefight

There was nothing the county sheriff and his posse could do to prevent the outrage visited on the village of Goldsboro. It was January 15, 1867, and hundreds of criminals had flocked into town on the railroad to make mischief and to watch the prizefight. Bullies, thieves, gamblers and pickpockets gathered in one unruly mass, armed to the teeth with knives and revolvers.

The rampage had started even before the mob hit town, with desperadoes hijacking trains leaving Baltimore and New York City. They plundered fellow passengers, heaping abuse and insult on anybody with whom they

Vintage photo of a Goldsboro street scene. *From the collection of the York County Heritage Trust, York, Pennsylvania.*

came into contact. "No one within their reach was safe," the *York Gazette* reported. Their outrage extended to every stop along the way, and in two or three cases, they threw people from the train at rail stations.

Sheriff Engles thought it prudent to have a posse on the ground early in the morning of January 15, but he and his men were laughed at and dismissed by the mob, estimated at about one thousand. "Their efforts to preserve the public peace were all in vain," the *Gazette* reported.

The newspaper *True Democrat* compared what happened next to the 1863 invasion by the Confederates. Local residents stayed at home "perfectly paralyzed and panic stricken," while the intruders had "matters all their own way." The newspaper described how "the Baltimore roughs" barged into homes and robbed people on the street. "They conducted themselves in the most indecent and disorderly manner…No one dared to resist them. The bout attracted hundreds of as godless and abandoned a set of scamps as ever disgraced the soul of humanity."

The fight between Sam Collyer of Baltimore and John McGlade of New York started at about 11:00 a.m. and continued for fifty-two grueling minutes. Collyer suffered only slight damage and was declared the winner after forty-seven rounds. McGlade, however, left the ring with a broken

This wood engraving from 1858 depicts spectators watching the prizefight between John Morrissey and John C. Heenan, aka the Benica Boy. *Courtesy of the Library of Congress.*

rib and a badly mangled face. The Baltimore fans came away victorious, heading home with more than $200,000 in winnings—the modern equivalent of about $3,080,000.

Among those placing wagers was a deputy sheriff from Philadelphia along with several politicians, including the notorious John Morrissey. The *True Democrat* reported how the "roughs and bob tails of New York" had elected this hoodlum turned bare-fisted brawler to Congress the previous fall. The newspaper had this to say in criticism of Morrissey: "He took an active part, betting his money freely on the result…A proper carrying out indeed of his virtuous intentions some time expressed in reference to himself and his family."

The mob resumed its brutal behavior on the trip home to Maryland and New York. With the criminals gone, Goldsboro recovered, but newspapers kept alive the need for justice. The *True Democrat*, on January 22, called on readers to pressure authorities to avenge "a most disgraceful scene" enacted within county limits and indict those who destroyed property and heaped insults on respectable ladies: "Our reputation was put in jeopardy, our safety menaced and our moral sense highly insulted. Let the grand jury…teach all lawless desperadoes that we are sensitive of our honor and jealous of our reputation."

The same edition also vowed that history would not repeat itself and that next time the authorities will be ready to put down such an outrage and arrest those responsible on the spot:

> *This is the first and…last time our county will be disgraced by such an unexampled display of rowdyism…If Morrissey and his cohorts desire to keep these exhibitions, we trust they would confine their operations to New York where people were accustomed to them and not make the soil of Pennsylvania the theater of their unblushing defiance of law and order…Otherwise, we assure them they will not escape again the will and the power of our people.*

The rowdiness spilled over into other communities. The *York County Star* in Wrightsville reported that some inhabitants of the "usually peaceful town" became belligerent after having "caught the infection" from the recent Goldsboro affair. Several fights broke out on the southern part of town, with one or two involving cases of "considerable pummeling" and another where the loser took unspecified legal action.

Local newspapers reported how Engles tried to recruit help from the Zeigle Guards, a military company that was heading for Harrisburg for the inauguration of John W. Greary as Pennsylvania governor. The sheriff met up with the troop at its depot in York and stated his determination to stop the fight if possible. The unit commander agreed to help and even dispatched soldiers to gather ammunition, but the unit was never used to disperse the fight.

The *True Democrat*, in its January 29 edition, ran a correction stating that the unit's lack of participation was the result of a misunderstanding. Upon arriving at Goldsboro, the sheriff and his posse left the train to reconnoiter the town. The newspaper reported that while Engles intended to ask for help, he didn't formally request military assistance. Blame was fixed on the conductor, who didn't wait for Engles to confirm whether intervention was needed and ordered the train to depart for Harrisburg with the Zeigle Guards.

"We make this correction cheerfully in justice to the guards who were ready to serve the sheriff," the article read, adding how the soldiers were disappointed they were not called into action.

"Fatal Lack of Continuity": The Pleasureville Brawl

The mystery man stalked her dream of Pleasureville. Susan Dellinger could feel his presence on the fringe of her perception. Yet this mother of fourteen children was not afraid. She was determined to recover the missing revolver of eighteen-year-old William Hoover. "It was on my right side and I wanted to go after it, but I…heard a man coming near me," she described her dream to police. "I kept on going, hoping he would…pass beyond and let me finish my search unmolested, but he seemed to keep right after me. I could not get rid of my unseen companion."

She had walked a fair distance down Emigsville Road before backtracking to the crime scene. The man followed her closely, as though content only to unnerve the woman and not to do her harm. She pressed on and saw the revolver again, this time to her left but in the same spot as before—lying atop the tombstone of Curtis Sipe in the old churchyard. In her earlier dream, this was where she saw Henry Snyder toss the handgun he had taken from William only three nights before. It was located half a block from where the victims were found mortally wounded and lying in pools of frozen blood on November 17, 1907. Her tip would later lead to the discovery of the revolver by her seventeen-year-old son George.

As the story goes, George Dellinger was walking down Emigsville Road when he saw four boys from the village hunting for the revolver in a field beyond the churchyard. He had just gone over the fence and took eight steps when he saw the rusted handgun right in front of him about 250 feet north of the crime scene. Discovery of the weapon confirmed police suspicions that Snyder had acted alone in the double homicide of William and his fifteen-year-old brother Curvin.

Newspaper sketch of the Pleasureville brawl crime scene. *Reprinted by permission of the* York Daily Record/York Sunday News.

Susan Dellinger was hesitant at first to discuss her two dreams with the police, leery of the notoriety it would give her. Strange how the dreams took place during a fitful night's rest before she even knew that the revolver was missing. Dellinger felt sorry for the parents of the Hoover brothers, who had often visited her sons. Mourning their deaths must have triggered the dreams about the revolver. Police saw it as a remarkable coincidence. Nothing more was said in newspaper reports of the mystery man who haunted her second dream.

When Snyder learned that the revolver had been found, he asked Chief of Detectives Charles White to come to his jail cell. "I told you if you look, you'll find the gun," Snyder told White just before he confessed again to killing the brothers, changing his story slightly to account for the revolver.

"When they came to me, I shot Curvin, and then I shot William," Snyder said. "I took his revolver from inside his coat pocket and kept it until I got to the edge of the woods and threw it away. I threw it to my right-hand side. Did they find it there?" By then, Snyder had changed his story half a dozen times about how he had murdered the Hoover boys. Police began their investigation after Henry Seiple discovered their bodies as he was driving a horse and buggy from Pleasureville to Emigsville at about 6:30 a.m. on November 17.

At first, Seiple thought that he saw the bodies of dead dogs when he happened to glance down the side street next to the United Brethren Church

This photograph taken by the author shows the crime scene as it appears today. The bodies of the Hoover brothers were found in proximity to where the car is cresting the hill. *Photo by Joseph Cress.*

graveyard on the outskirts of Pleasureville. He took a closer look and saw two men lying on the road. Thinking that they were drunk, Seiple went to the home of Bert Sipe, and together they returned to the scene with a lantern intent on rousing the boys from their stupor. Instead, they were shocked to find two boys barely alive and unconscious, their bodies frozen to the ground. Both had suffered a single gunshot wound to the head.

The alarm was raised, and villagers arrived on the scene. They carried the brothers to a nearby barbershop, where they quickly determined that Curvin was beyond help. The boy would later die at home at about 12:30 p.m. As for William, he was rushed to York Hospital, but efforts to save him also proved futile. He was far too weak to undergo surgery and died at about 6:45 p.m. But before he was transported, rescuers tried to revive him by repeatedly bathing his head and briskly rubbing his hands. William opened his eyes briefly, long enough for the barber to ask, "Were you hit from the back with a club?" William said no. "Were you shot?" William answered yes before he passed out again and never regained consciousness.

Twenty-two-year-old Henry Snyder of Pleasureville was among the first to see the brothers lying prostrate on the barbershop floor. A witness would later testify that the killer clasped a hand from each brother before falling to his knees and shedding tears for his companions. At first, Snyder told no one that he was the shooter, including Mrs. Hoover, whom he had volunteered to drive home. He did, however, correct her on the precise location of where her sons were found as they drove past the crime scene. At the barbershop, Henry told his father Frank that he was with the brothers the night of the shooting but denied any knowledge of what had happened to them.

Police were baffled at first by the apparent apathy of Pleasureville residents. Gunfire was heard by at least a dozen people, yet no one bothered to investigate, so the victims were left to bleed out slowly for six hours before their bodies were found. Police were told that gunfire in the village was so common at night that it attracted little attention.

Reverend M.J. Heberly was sleeping in the corner bedroom of the parsonage located at the intersection of Emigsville Road and the main street through Pleasureville. At about 11:45 p.m. on November 16, he was awakened by a jumble of angry words spoken by men talking loudly outside his window. Peering out, he saw one man in a buggy along with three to four others standing on the ground. "If Henry did not treat you right" were the only words that Heberly was able to understand. He believed that the words were spoken by Snyder's friend, seventeen-year-old Lester Kauffman.

The noise died down, so Heberly returned to bed, only to be roused again by four gunshots fired in rapid succession, followed a minute later by two more shots. Due to the rapid pattern, Heberly did not associate the first four shots with a crime. He figured that it was just a drunk at the crossroads firing a handgun into the air. The fifth and sixth shots were spaced farther apart and originated farther down the Emigsville Road just behind and to the east of the parsonage. Still, the pastor concluded that the gunfire was in the spirit of fun, so he returned to bed, never suspecting that there were two bodies on the road.

Henry Smyser was driving an eastbound buggy through Pleasureville on his way to Starview when he heard gunfire echo through the streets. As Smyser passed the intersection, he saw two boys standing at the corner looking down Emigsville Road at what he thought was a drunk lying on the ground. Pressing on, Smyser saw Kauffman and eighteen-year-old Oscar Hoover riding in a buggy bound for their homes in Starview. It was unclear in the newspaper reports whether Oscar was related to the victims. Meanwhile, John Innerst was walking down the main street of Pleasureville when he heard gunfire and saw a muzzle flash as he passed the parsonage corner and looked down Emigsville Road. He then saw a man stagger and fall but thought that the person was drunk. Innerst walked home rather than get involved.

The investigation led police to charge Snyder, Kauffman and Oscar Hoover with first-degree murder. Testimony would later establish that the trio was returning home from a night of barhopping in York when they encountered the Hoover brothers at a store in Pleasureville. The brothers then accompanied the suspects on a buggy ride to the church intersection, where they, along with Snyder, parted ways from Kauffman and Oscar Hoover just before midnight. There was a theory that an argument took place during the buggy ride between Snyder and Kauffman and that the Hoover brothers, who were believed to be sober, tried to intervene.

From the start, police believed that Snyder was their strongest suspect. His multiple versions of what happened hurt his credibility, plus he had confessed early on to firing his revolver that night. In an early statement to police, Snyder implicated Kauffman, claiming that his one-time friend stood up in the buggy and shouted, "I'll fix him!" at Snyder before firing the fatal shots. A different version by Snyder had either Kauffman or Oscar Hoover firing handguns without warning from the buggy at the men standing on the ground. In both cases, Snyder said that he fired back in defense, hitting no one.

Snyder once told police that Curvin was hit accidentally by one of the four rapid-fire shots. A slightly different version had William accidentally shooting his brother before he himself was shot by Snyder. In both cases, Snyder said that he pulled the trigger in self-defense after an enraged William charged him while holding either a stone or a revolver. This begged the question: what happened to the victim's handgun? Snyder said that he didn't know where it was but said that police could probably find it if they conducted a search.

Gradually, Snyder added a shot of alcohol to his story, claiming that he had purchased whiskey on his way home for the Hoover brothers and had arranged to meet up with them in Pleasureville the night of the shootings. After they parted ways with Lester and Oscar, Snyder gave the brothers the whiskey they had asked for, but Snyder claimed that they wanted more. They believed that he was holding out on them, so they tried to frisk his clothing. At that point, Snyder pushed Curvin away and shot the younger brother. He then shot William to prevent the older brother from talking to authorities.

The many conflicting stories only made police suspect that Snyder was trying to shield himself by lying about his friends. Eventually, the commonwealth dropped the murder charges against Lester Kauffman and Oscar Hoover, releasing both men on bail so they could later testify during the April 1908 trial of Henry Snyder. They told jurors that each of the trio had consumed at least six glasses of beer in York, along with some whiskey on the way home. Both men testified to saying goodbye to Snyder and the Hoover brothers before leaving without incident.

When Snyder took the stand in his own defense, he testified that he was at the church that night and heard gunfire but didn't know who fired the shots or from what direction. Snyder claimed that he saw two boys traveling on the Emigsville Road but didn't know their identities. When asked if he shot the Hoover brothers, Snyder answered, "Not that I know of." The prosecution entered his latest confession as evidence, and the jury found Snyder guilty of first-degree murder.

Attorneys for Snyder tried to use epilepsy as an insanity defense. They claimed that he had suffered from frequent seizures from when he was eight months until thirteen years old. This had the effect of arresting his intellectual development. Snyder was twice the normal age when he learned to talk and was often a large boy in a class with small children. By age eight, he had suffered as many as twenty-five seizures in a single year, but few outside the family ever witnessed the spasms because his parents kept Henry at home. Finally, they withdrew him from school in despair.

Newspaper sketch of the courtroom during the Pleasureville brawl murder trial. *Reprinted by permission of the* York Daily Record/York Sunday News.

Snyder had also suffered trauma when his head was run over by a wagon wheel when he was a boy.

His attorneys argued that epilepsy created within Snyder an uncontrollable impulse to vent the violence building up inside of him. The large quantity of alcohol Snyder drank the night of the shootings wore down his resistance to expressing that violence. They wanted to call experts to prove their theory, but the judge rejected their argument, saying that there was a "fatal lack of continuity" between the last major seizure and the mental state of the accused at the time of the shooting. Defense attorneys could not produce a doctor who had any record or memory of treating epilepsy in Snyder.

Together with his family and friends, the attorneys were more successful in saving Snyder from the gallows. They submitted petitions signed by hundreds of county residents asking the board of pardons to commute the death sentence to life imprisonment. Snyder supporters based their request on him being drunk the night of the shootings. They argued that while Snyder was not legally insane, he was "mentally weak, lacking perception and apprehension."

The board took up the case on September 28, 1909, by hearing testimony from expert witnesses who had opinions on Snyder's mental state. His attorneys argued that while the conviction was proper Snyder deserved leniency. On October 21, 1909, the *York Gazette* reported how the pardons board had granted Snyder a reprieve and that he would not be executed the following Tuesday.

When asked for comment, Snyder appeared as sulky and indifferent as he had during trial and refused, at first, to make any direct statement to the newspaper. When the sheriff asked Snyder if he would sleep better, Snyder answered with quivering lips, "I can sleep better if those who put me here can." He agreed with the sheriff that his attorneys did everything in their power to save his life. Snyder was a model prisoner but had few friends including the sheriff.

"The board of pardons has proved itself to be a board of mercy," said defense attorney John Hoober. "For the sake of the unfortunate boy, for the sake of a frail mother and for the sake of a father, whose stalwart frame I have seen a rock in agonized distress, I am overjoyed the efforts long continued have come to this happy ending."

"The Frenzy of Terror": The Church Panic of 1907

Silence hung heavy among the crowd gathered at Quickel Lutheran Church to mourn the passing of William and Curvin Hoover. It was November 20, 1907—three days after the brothers were found mortally wounded in Pleasureville. Two thousand people crammed the auditorium and balcony of the one-story building that measured about forty-five feet wide and sixty feet long. Most came out of sympathy for the family of the popular boys, but others no doubt were just morbidly curious.

The slow, steady peal of the church bell made for a sad refrain to the weeping heard throughout the sanctuary from the grieving parents. The casket lids had been removed to allow mourners one last glimpse of the two brothers who were shot through the head by Henry Snyder. As people waited for the funeral service to begin, fear and worry took residence in their hearts.

It began as they entered the church when someone commented how overcrowding could endanger the structure. This circulated as a rumor whispered among the crowd until one person reported it to Reverend Adam Stump, the church pastor. He tried unsuccessfully to clear the building before the service began at noon. Ten minutes into the funeral, Stump was on his feet, telling mourners that there was no immediate danger, when someone shouted, "The roof is falling!" That same moment, there was the sound of creaking timbers and two unlit stoves overturning. A reporter described what happened next: "In an instant the solemn throng was transformed into a rampant mob dominated by the frenzy of terror and brute instinct of self-

Photograph of the Quickel Evangelical Lutheran Church as it appears today in Zions View. *Photo by Joseph Cress.*

preservation. The shouting and struggling mass of humanity presented a spectacle that was harrowing."

An editorial published the next day in the *York Dispatch* theorized that the mourners "were keyed up…to an unusual tension" by the emotion of the double homicide. The writer felt that the combination of the warning shout and creaking timbers spread fear among those gathered. He presented the following eyewitness account and analysis:

> *Scores tried to squeeze through doorways and, becoming wedged, blocked the now frenzied crowd struggling desperately within. Most panics in buildings are alike in one respect. The crowd seems to lose all idea of reason. Impelled by the dread of death, they become unconsciously brutal in their efforts to escape the impending doom.*

Men, women and children were trampled in the crush of humanity making for the narrow exits. At the height of the frenzy, Frank Hoover, father of the murdered boys, stood beside his wife and daughter in front of the coffins—ready as a family to protect the bodies from desecration. Local undertaker John Bahn suffered internal injuries and a badly cut and sprained left wrist while trying to keep the coffins from being overthrown. A reporter described the scene: "The surging mass…crowded him to one side and one coffin containing the body of the younger boy [Curvin] was thrown to the floor and broken. The corpse was also thrown out, but many of the cooler heads soon had the body replaced and the upturned casket again set on the supports."

It is believed that Mrs. George Renner of York, the boys' aunt, was the first person hurt in the panic. Seated near the center of the auditorium, she was shoved out of the aisle, thrown to the floor and trampled upon by those fighting to reach an exit. In the process, she lost consciousness, but her husband managed to get her near a window, where she was resuscitated before being rescued. She was not alone. William Stauffer of Wellsville and Lester Gross of Zions View—both seven-year-old boys—were severely injured after being trampled underfoot. Stauffer suffered a concussion and bruises, while Gross had internal injuries and bruising to the chest.

Some mourners, in their desperation, leaped out of windows, only to be jumped on by those following. A large man, in his bid for safety, dove through a closed window, taking the sash and everything else with him. Journalists were unable to learn his name—only that he was cut by the glass and left a blood trail behind. It is believed that Mrs. Daniel March of North York was the most seriously injured victim of the panic. Her right leg was broken in several places, and her body was badly bruised when she tried to leave through a window. She was carried to a nearby residence, where she suffered great pain as she waited for a doctor to arrive.

Maternal instinct kicked in as women tried desperately to protect their children. One lady saved her infant by thrusting it into the arms of a newspaper man who had left through a window. Other women threw their children out of low windows or fought hard to get back into the church once they realized that they had become separated. Many women bore up well through the ordeal until they got outside, where they fainted on the lawn.

The many cries for help echoed through the village of Zions View, drawing a large crowd to the church. Inside, pastors Stump and George Enders stayed at the pulpit "loudly admonishing the multitude to be calm and exercise judgment," according to the newspaper. Just as they were able to restore some semblance of order, someone raised the alarm again, causing people on the balcony to panic and jump onto those still struggling to break free from the auditorium. Other mourners were thrown down stairs. Before this second alarm, the people on the balcony were leaving in a relatively orderly fashion. Several more minutes would pass before the church was empty and calm restored. The pastors were the last ones to leave.

The church panic lasted about ten minutes, during which more than fifty people were injured, including twelve seriously. Most suffered cuts and bruises. The majority of injuries took place near the rear door, which was the narrowest exit. At one point, the bodies here were piled several deep. The evacuation completed, the focus shifted to the injured as phone calls were made to summon doctors to the scene.

The aftermath left the church interior cluttered with overturned and splintered pews along with apparel strewn across the floor. "Many people had clothing torn from their backs," a reporter wrote. "Enough pocketbooks, watches, combs, hats, coats, handkerchiefs and other articles littered the floor to fill a cart." The exhaust pipes from the overturned stoves were trampled into flat sheets of metal by the panicking crowd.

In the ensuing investigation, no one could trace the initial cry of "The roof is falling" to any particular individual. Police officials and journalists attending the funeral were approached minutes before the panic by men who claimed that the roof was sagging. The men felt that the support beams were under great strain from the weight of so many people. R.S. Stahle, a local doctor, told investigators that he had information from reliable sources that the structure was unsafe. Yet when Stahle and some other men inspected the building after the panic, they found everything to be structurally sound. "The building may have settled, the walls may have bulged and the roof sagged at the time, but later retained their normal condition," Stahle said. "I'm afraid the result would have been more terrible had all those people remained inside."

Church officials maintained that the building was perfectly safe and only damaged during the panic. The architectural firm of Hamme & Laber thoroughly inspected the church before issuing a statement verifying that the building was safe and could be used without fear. "We have been unable to find the slightest evidence of structural weakness in floors, walls or roof," the statement read. Built in 1850, the church still stands today in Conewago Township more than a century after the incident.

The panic put an abrupt end to the funeral service inside the church, but the ceremony continued outside, attended by only a handful of the original mourners. Within half an hour of the panic, pallbearers had carried the caskets from the church to the adjoining cemetery, where the brothers were buried. Enders began the graveside service with a prayer of comfort for the families of both the murdered boys and the suspects in custody for the double homicide. He then condemned alcohol consumption in minors by saying, "May the rising generations of children learn the lesson of temperance, caution and all that tends to preserve the mind."

In his funeral sermon, Stump criticized the role that alcohol had played in the murders. Trial testimony would establish how an intoxicated Henry Snyder shot the Hoover brothers before midnight on November 16, 1907. To Stump, "all those who have anything to do with the liquor traffic...are murderers in the sight of God." He praised Pleasureville residents for keeping their village dry: "For all the wickedness that is said to abound in Pleasureville and remarks about its character which have been going around, there are not twelve men in the whole town who would sign a liquor license. May the Lord God paralyze any man who would dare to establish a hell-hole saloon in the town of Pleasureville."

Stump also defended the honor of the Hoover brothers while expressing support for the death penalty. Here are some excerpts:

Reverend Adam Stump, circa 1920. *From the collection of the York County Heritage Trust, York, Pennsylvania.*

> *Who are the victims? They were peaceful and of a friendly disposition. There was no proof they ever picked a quarrel with anyone. They were at Pleasureville on an errand to make purchases and also spend several social hours with their companions...The facts of this fearful tragedy are staring us in the face. They are plain and not much effort is required to solve the mystery...The man who kills should not be permitted to live...Those who hold life cheap are acting against the wishes of God himself...He takes it as an insult and has declared their life shall be forfeited either by decapitation, hanging, the electric chair or any other manner of death.*

In addition, Stump spoke out on shortcomings he saw in the legal system. Any lawyer who clears a guilty client on a technicality is as guilty of murder as the defendant, he said. He felt the same of any jury that clears a man on obvious evidence or of any citizen who declines to testify in a capital case.

Stump mentioned how he had visited Lester Kauffman, Henry Snyder and Oscar Hoover in jail, hoping that the three suspects in the double homicide would tell the truth about what happened. Stump figured that confession was not only good for the soul but also their only hope of salvation. Instead, Stump was foiled in his effort to get at the truth by defense attorneys who had instructed the suspects not to talk about the case. This did not prevent Stump from issuing a warning: "The habit of carrying a pistol...and having a riotous good time are too prevalent among our young men. There is not a parent in York not in danger of having his son come home with blood upon his soul or of having a daughter outraged. Where are your children in the late hours of the night?"

"THE NARROW PATH": LAST CALL FOR "PEGGY" LARUE

What can be more blind—love or Lady Justice? Fred McLean was alone again with his intended victim as he waited for a taxicab to take him from the courthouse to York County Prison. The prizefighter known as "Sailor Kid Mack" had just been convicted of second-degree murder, but his sweetheart Nora O'Bryan thought him lucky. The longest sentence her lover could receive was twenty years in state prison. Something of her beauty was taken away on August 9, 1924, when McLean shot a bullet through her cheek that became embedded in her neck near the spinal cord. What the couple talked about in that office was not reported in the newspaper, only that the crippled

Exterior view of the York County Courthouse. *Photo by Joseph Cress.*

woman "radiated happiness" and that, when the talk ended, they parted with a fond kiss. The date was January 9, 1925.

Only the day before, the morbidly curious had gathered in the courtroom in eager anticipation of O'Bryan's testimony. They figured that the twenty-eight-year-old woman would break down and cry just as she had at other times during the trial, but they were disappointed. Limping, she leaned on her mother's arm as the two women, neatly dressed in black, made their way to the witness stand, where Nora surprised many with her composure. One reporter observed: "She proved the truth of the saying—women in times of great stress or in big moments hold their nerve better than men."

She only faltered once, when her eyes began to tear up near the end of her testimony. A court attendant gave her a drink of water, which seemed to help. Nora described how early on the morning of August 6, 1924, she was at a party drunk on moonshine in a field off the Carlisle Road about a mile outside York.

She testified how she took a revolver from McLean's hip pocket and stuck it in her stocking. Dazed, McLean woke from his stupor, angry over the theft. He demanded his gun back. She threw it back at him, urging him to put it away before someone gets hurt. The next thing she remembered was that a bullet had struck her in the cheek and she had fallen to the ground unconscious.

McLean fired a second bullet, which struck twenty-four-year-old Alice May Abbott as she was passed out and prone on the ground. This bullet entered the back of Abbott's neck near the base of her skull and severed the spinal cord. A prostitute, Abbott (alias Carmen "Peggy" Larue), died instantly, leading police to charge McLean with her murder. Before his shooting spree was over, the boxer would also wound David Dorwart of Lancaster before turning the gun on himself in a botched suicide attempt. When McLean testified at his trial, "[H]e blubbered like a child in answering the questions of his [defense] counsel James Glessner," a reporter wrote. "[McLean] lost all of his bravado and became a pitiable creature on the witness stand."

McLean could not recall events from the time he fell asleep in the field after drinking the moonshine until he woke up at York Hospital. He denied making the statements attributed to him by other witnesses but admitted that he owned the revolver used in the shooting. McLean said that he had bought the handgun four days before the incident, claiming that he needed it for protection in Maryland, where he was absent without leave from an army post. In his closing statement, District Attorney Amos Herrmann argued that there was no evidence McLean had consumed any more alcohol than Dorwart or O'Bryan, yet he was the only one forgetful of events. Herrmann noted how clear McLean's memory was in recalling his military service along with his record as a bantamweight boxing champion in the Hawaiian Islands.

Originally set for October 1924, the trial had to be delayed two months until the injured were well enough to testify. The most difficult surgery was to remove the bullet from O'Bryan's neck because of its proximity to the spinal cord. The bullet that hit McLean was found under his left shoulder blade and removed by surgery performed with a local anesthetic. Dorwart was thought to be the least wounded of the three survivors, yet his recovery was the slowest due to infection and the danger of blood poisoning.

The January term of York County Court seemed jinxed at first. Kathryn Millar, a material witness for the prosecution, failed to appear for the McLean trial, requiring deputy sheriffs to track her to New Oxford, where she was found nursing a sick uncle. She had written the wrong court date on her calendar. That same day, E. Milton Stambaugh, formerly of Spring Grove, collapsed in the courtroom and was carried by tipstaff to Herrmann's office, where he later died of an apparent heart attack. Another man was overcome by epileptic fits and had to be assisted downstairs, where he later recovered.

Vintage postcard of the old York Hospital on West College Street. *From the collection of the York County Heritage Trust, York, Pennsylvania.*

Nurse Millar was in charge of the York Hospital ward where McLean was being treated for his self-inflicted wound. She testified how he had expressed regret for killing Larue when it was his intention to kill O'Bryan. He explained how he had acquired the revolver about a week before the shooting. This confession came several hours after McLean was admitted to the hospital, and Millar could still smell liquor on his breath. She relayed what was said to police detective Charles White, who then interviewed McLean directly.

The boxer admitted that the revolver belonged to him and again said that he was sorry for Larue. He had nothing against her or Dorwart but was tired of O'Bryan running after him and annoying him, so he decided to shoot her. At trial, his attorney moved to have the testimony of Millar stricken from the record on the grounds that McLean had not been advised that anything he would say could be used against him. The court overruled the motion and allowed the confession to be admitted.

David Dorwart, star witness for the prosecution, appeared weak and pale on the stand from his long hospital stay. His right hand covered in bandages, Dorwart testified that he had left his home in Lancaster at about 11:30 p.m. the night of the shooting. He then drove to Columbia, Lancaster County, where he met up with Larue, and together they went to the Crystal Restaurant in York city for something to eat. There, they linked up with McLean and O'Bryan before heading over to a home on the south side of town, where they each drank four to six shots of liquor. They then left for an early morning joyride into the outskirts, taking along moonshine in soda bottles.

They drove out West Market Street before turning onto the Carlisle Road. "Peggy was drunk," Dorwart told jurors. "We thought if we got her out in the open, it would be better for her." They parked in a field, where Dorwart and Larue exited the car while McLean and O'Bryan stayed inside. At some point, McLean fell asleep, and Dorwart saw O'Bryan remove the gun from his pocket and put it in her stocking. When McLean woke up and found the revolver gone, he immediately accused O'Bryan of taking it. A fight developed in which McLean hit O'Bryan several times, throwing her to the ground. Sailor Mack then took the handgun from her stocking just before she leaped to her feet. He opened fire, hitting the two women.

This scared Dorwart, who threw his right hand into the air as he ran from the scene. The third bullet caught Dorwart in the palm and became embedded near his right wrist. Dorwart escaped to a nearby farm, where he got help. Meanwhile, McLean turned the gun on himself and fired one round, which entered his chest about an inch above and to the left of his heart. The bullet pierced his left lung and became lodged in his back.

Paul Strickler of Dover was on his way to Baltimore when he saw McLean run out into the road at about 5:20 a.m. He stopped his car to help. Before showing Strickler his chest wound, McLean confessed to shooting the two women and refused an offer for a ride back into York. Strickler climbed into his car and left to report the incident to police. A second motorist, Frank Knisely, also stopped to help McLean, who again refused a ride to the hospital. "The Hell with me, you go get the women," McLean reportedly said as he brushed away tears. The wounded boxer kept swearing at Knisely, urging him to help the women, until he finally relented and allowed Knisely to drive him to the hospital.

At trial, Herrmann pushed for a first-degree murder conviction, arguing that there was still premeditation even though McLean had failed to kill his intended target. This makes him just as guilty and does not lessen the degree of murder, Herrmann told jurors. Here is an excerpt from his closing statement: "With the coming of dawn, there came the angel of death for that woman unprepared to meet her death unforgiven of her sins. She died at the hands of one who had no right to take her. He is the two-fisted man who slaps women and then kills them. He is the man responsible."

The jury took about eight hours to find McLean guilty of second-degree murder. On their first ballot, members of the jury were unanimous in their rejection of a first-degree murder conviction. It took four more ballots and hours of discussion for them to arrive at the final decision.

The true identity of Carmen "Peggy" Larue was initially a mystery to authorities until an investigation by Coroner L.U. Zech revealed her double life. She was found in the field next to O'Bryan when police arrived on the scene. Larue was described as an attractive woman with bobbed auburn hair who wore jewelry and gold earrings. The victim was married to William Abbott of Peterson, New Jersey, and was the mother of two small children. She was regarded as respectable until 1920, when she "developed a penchant for running around," reported the *York Gazette and Daily*. "She left the narrow path because of her infatuation for another man."

That man was William Snyder, a justice of the peace, who was eventually charged with embezzling bail money. In 1922, the victim abandoned her family to run away with Snyder to Canada, where they stayed until his funds ran low. The couple then moved to New York, where Snyder worked as a barber and "Alice May Abbott" worked in a restaurant. Snyder was caught, convicted of the charges and sentenced on May 16, 1924, to one to three years in the New Jersey state prison. In her personal effects, investigators found letters addressed to "Peggy Snyder Larue" and signed "From your husband-to-be, William Snyder." She wrote letters back addressed to Snyder.

In early June 1924, William Abbott received a note from his estranged wife, who wanted to see her children again and asked if she could visit. By that time, he had disowned her, so he ignored her request. He later told investigators that, after forsaking her family, his wife trained as a nurse and worked for some time in Buffalo, New York, and later at a village for epileptics in Skillman, New Jersey. He discredited her story about being a college graduate and a chemistry expert.

That was the story Mrs. Abbott had used about two weeks before her murder, when she first arrived at a whorehouse in Columbia, Lancaster County. When interviewed by investigators, the madam felt certain that Abbott, alias Carmen Larue, was new to the oldest profession. This seemed to be confirmed by the borough police chief, who remembered seeing the victim cowering in the corner of one room during a recent raid on the brothel. Upon her murder, hundreds of people viewed the body of Mrs. Abbott dressed in a nurse's uniform and laid out in an oak casket. Her remains were later shipped to Hawthorne, New Jersey, for burial.

PART III
THE PERILS OF PARAMOURS

Love and obsession often go hand in hand in a marriage divorced of all reason. Soon the person we long to cherish becomes an object we struggle to control. It is when love turns toxic that passion stirs to violence and blood begins to flow. In the pages that follow, you will read about how a habitual lady killer preyed on married women until jealousy took his life. You will also witness a boy in a man's body throw a temper tantrum at being rejected one too many times. But no romance turned horror show would be complete without a sordid cast of supporting characters, including loathsome body snatchers, crusading Klansmen and heartless fans of capital punishment.

"Unsound Mind": Lost Loves of Johnny Coyle

John Coyle Sr. was ready when the body snatchers came for his son. Several men had waited for the cover of night to trespass on the family homestead in Hellem Township. The father saw them turn in the direction of the grave that he had dug under an apple tree overlooking the Susquehanna River. With shotgun in hand, John Sr. was tired of this humiliation. Earlier that day, his only son had been executed in a public spectacle. So when the ghouls drew closer, he fired a single burst, hitting no one but scaring the intruders back into the darkness. The *York Press*, in its coverage, urged an end to the harassment. The newspaper thought that people had gone too far: "Considerable indignation and excitement arises from this attempt to

The grave site of Johnny Coyle, located along the Susquehanna River. *Photo by Joseph Cress.*

disturb the remains of the hanged murderer…The general verdict is that they should be allowed to rest in peace."

On April 22, 1884, time was almost up for John Coyle Jr. Thousands had gathered in Gettysburg to witness his public hanging, but admission to the jail yard was limited. Scalpers sold tickets for as much as five dollars for a close-up view of a killer's final moments. By then, his elderly parents had suffered through two murder trials and several unsuccessful attempts to spare his life. A reporter captured this final tender moment of bitter departure: "The old grey heads bowed over his shoulders embracing him as only parents can embrace a child…Hot tears of deep grief rolling fast and thick down their wrinkled cheeks."

It had been almost three years since their twenty-seven-year-old son had walked into the cattle barn on the family homestead shortly after 5:00 a.m. on May 30, 1881. Coyle went there to confront the woman he professed to love with yet another marriage proposal. Described as young and raven-haired, Emily Myers was busy milking the cows. An orphan from Chambersburg, she had worked for the family for about a year. Myers needed the money, and the elderly couple needed the help.

When propositioned several times before, Myers always refused, saying that she was not ready for marriage. She insisted that Johnny leave her alone.

Yet this time, when Myers said no, Coyle pulled out a pistol and shot her through the heart, killing her instantly before he turned the pistol on himself. Using powder and paper wadding, Johnny inflicted superficial head wounds in what investigators believe was an attempt to win the sympathy of others.

Mary and John Sr. ran a ferry crossing connecting Wrightsville to Marietta. Their inn was a popular resort along the river for sportsmen and gamblers from the surrounding area. Sources describe their son as one of the best ferrymen of his time, "knowing every pothole and shallow for a mile up and down the landings." Most everyone thought of him as a simple-minded person with a fondness for alcohol and a history of erratic behavior.

The mother testified that Johnny had always been moody and unhappy and showed signs of insanity and foolishness since he was a boy. It was clear that he was different from other children. One time, he accidentally shot himself while duck hunting and then anguished over becoming a cripple.

"His father and I had a great deal of difficulty restraining him—he almost went crazy with worry," Mary Coyle said. Her husband testified how their son became "morbidly sensitive" after the gunshot wound and after he suffered from typhoid fever for about three months in 1874. John Sr. believed that this combined with alcoholism drove his son into a melancholy, which worsened his strange behavior. "A physician said we should take care of our son or he would lose his mind entirely," the father said.

They took their son to two doctors, but none of the prescribed treatments seemed to work for Johnny, who often walked off alone and disappeared for days at a time. The couple was so concerned that they offered a man room and board to watch over their son for a winter. There were other halfhearted tries at suicide before the day he shot himself after killing Myers. In 1876, Mary caught her son in the barn preparing to shoot himself. "My brother called to him. John dropped the pistol. [He] looked haggard and crazy." There was also the time when her son carried a razor and threatened to slash his own throat.

The day of the murder, Mary was calling for Emily when her son walked in with blood running out of his ears and down his breast. "He looked frightful," she told jurors. "Eyes large and glaring like fire." In confessing the crime, her son claimed that he went to the barn to see Myers and to verify her promise to marry him. "My son…told me that the girl had ruined him and set him crazy."

The first trial took place in October 1881 in a York County court and resulted in Johnny being found guilty of first-degree murder and sentenced to death by hanging. Defense attorneys did not challenge the prosecution's case

The Accomac Inn outside Wrightsville sits on the former location of the tavern operated by the Coyle family. *Photo by Joseph Cress.*

that Johnny was the gunman. Instead, their strategy was to prove a pattern of insanity since childhood that continued on through the commission of the crime. The goal was to show the jury that their client was not responsible for his actions.

Emily Robbins of Marietta was one of the defense witnesses called in support of this strategy. She testified that Johnny had once asked her to marry him, but she responded that she would only get married in a silk dress. Coyle offered his mother's dress and suggested that they marry that afternoon. "I did not think he was of sound mind," Robbins said, adding that she once saw him play marbles with young boys.

John Campbell, a hotel keeper in Marietta, always thought that Johnny was silly and foolish. "He would come from the post office to my place with love letters and asked me to read them or would read them aloud himself," Campbell said. "I often thought he wrote the letters." George Spangler of Marietta went hunting with Coyle years before the murder. Just as he was about to shoot a rabbit, Johnny threatened to shoot him if he shot the animal. "He had his gun pointed at me," Spangler recalled. "His eyes stood out."

Some witnesses did more to hinder than help the defense strategy. Henry Shad, publisher of the *Marietta Register*, testified that he overheard Coyle say after the murder, "My God, I wish I had shot and killed myself first, and then shot the girl." Shad concluded that Coyle had an unsound mind but was sane and knew the difference between right and wrong. Thus, he was responsible for his actions.

The prosecution relied on testimony that Coyle had threatened to shoot Myers before the murder and that afterward he had confessed to the crime. John Warfield told jurors that he had a talk with Coyle three days before the shooting as the suspect ferried him across the river.

"I want to get married, but have not got the means," Coyle told Warfield. "I have asked the maid twice and she has refused me. I intend to ask her again and if she refuses…by God, before she shall marry any other man, I will shoot her." Warfield tried to convince Johnny that this would only result in her death and his execution, but Coyle went on to say that whiskey and bad women have ruined him and that he didn't care anymore. The prosecution also called William Houck, who had transported Coyle to the York County jail the day of his arrest. The suspect told Houck that he had shot Myers after she rejected his marriage proposal and dared him to fire the gun. Coyle admitted that if he could not have Myers, he was determined that no one else would.

During the trial, the victim's sister sat at the prosecution's table, drawing all kinds of sympathy, even though there was no proof that the siblings were especially close. But perhaps the most dramatic moment was when the prosecution introduced as evidence the preserved heart of the victim, sealed in a jar, along with the dress she wore at the time of the shooting, with the hole plainly visible.

Following the first conviction, defense counsel took an appeal to the state Supreme Court, which heard the case in October 1882. The appeal argued that the York County judge, in his jury instructions, did not properly define the level of evidence needed to support an acquittal based on insanity. The high court clarified that there must be proof of habitual behavior and that care must be given not to confuse insanity with acts of reckless fury. The state court also granted Johnny a new trial, along with a request filed on his behalf for a change of venue.

On that, defense attorneys argued that the countywide publication of witness testimony from the first trial would make it difficult to obtain a fair jury for a second trial. Newspapers reported that the majority of York County residents had concluded that Coyle was guilty even before the first trial. An editorial writer even suggested that a trial was unnecessary and that the court should just condemn Coyle to the gallows.

The case was transferred to Gettysburg for the second murder trial. Hardly any new evidence had surfaced because the same witnesses testified again. On May 5, 1883, a jury took just three hours to convict Johnny of first-degree murder. A newspaper reporter, present in the courtroom, wrote: "The prisoner seemed unmoved as his aged mother burst into tears, 'Oh gentlemen, how could you take away my only son from me? May God forgive you for it.' The prisoner tried to console her, but she still cried bitterly."

At sentencing, the judge told Johnny that he had violated almost every commandment of moral law, including, "Honor thy father and mother." The bitter son replied that his father was to blame for not bringing him up properly or treating him right. The judge replied that this did not absolve him of guilt and recommended Coyle not trouble himself with the past but instead make peace with God.

It appeared that the condemned man followed that advice and reportedly converted to Christianity. Spiritual advisors visited him often in the weeks before the hanging, even as others continued to fight for his life. Friends and family recruited medical experts from Philadelphia who, after diagnosing Johnny insane, traveled to Harrisburg to plead his case. Coyle even wrote his own letter to Governor Robert Pattison in which he admitted to being weak-minded and prone to angry outbursts when drunk. His legal team thought that this could prompt the governor to issue a stay of execution. There was even speculation in Gettysburg that Coyle would cheat the hangman. But the governor decided not to intervene.

When told that there was no hope, Coyle fell to his knees and cried like a child, begging for mercy from the Adams County sheriff whom he had befriended while in jail. Feeling sympathetic, the sheriff offered Coyle a gill of alcohol to help him keep steady and meet his fate without flinching.

This may have been why Coyle mounted the platform with firm steps and kept his eyes focused on the ground. The sheriff's hand, however, was seen trembling slightly as he tied Johnny's legs together and placed the noose around his neck. As his final words, John Coyle Jr. forgave all of his enemies and said that he had no ill will against anyone. The black hood was put over his head, and the order given to release the trapdoor sending him into the afterlife.

The corpse was later placed in a coffin for transport by rail to the Hellam train station. There was a scene in the jail yard where a man displayed a small piece of the hangman's rope, which was cut up and distributed to spectators as souvenirs. Mary Coyle scolded the man, telling him that someday one of his children may be hanging from the gallows. Along the way, there were people who visited the railroad stations to get a glimpse of the coffin. The crowd in Hellam even asked the parents to open the coffin so that they could see the corpse. John Sr. refused, declaring "none of you false witnesses shall see Johnny."

"ONE SORROW AFTER ANOTHER": *THE PEOPLE V. ERVIN SPANGLER*

Harvey Smith was shocked at how something far colder than an early morning chill had seeped into the marrow of his bones. The snow was starting to fall when the truck driver reported for work at the C.E. Miller & Son Brickyard in York. In the dim light, he failed to notice how scarlet icicles hung from the bottom sill of what should have been a locked office door. The purity of white had barely concealed the wicked stain of the murderer's blood frozen as stiff as the wide-eyed corpse of Ervin "Jake" Spangler.

It was clear to Smith that his coworker must have taken the shotgun and placed the muzzle between his teeth before pulling the trigger. Horrified, Smith stepped gingerly over the crumpled remains on the floor and phoned the police. Spangler had scribbled the message "Goodbye to all" on the back of an envelope found in his pocket. Such was the end of a man who had killed two women and left six children motherless.

The discovery of the body at 7:30 a.m., December 17, 1932, concluded a manhunt that had started about 5:00 p.m. the day before, after police found Maude Rouscher face down on her kitchen floor. Her skull had been bashed in by seven blows from a hammer, and her throat had been cut clean through to the spinal column by a broken razor found in the sink. Her screams and the cries of her daughters alerted neighbors, who summoned police, but they were too late.

Investigators knew right away Spangler was the killer. He had been a frequent visitor to the home on School Alley where Rouscher and her children were staying from her estranged husband. That afternoon, nine-year-old Betty arrived home from school but was not allowed inside by Spangler, who insisted that she stay outside and play with her six-year-old sister, June. When Betty was refused a second time, she became frightened and suspected that something was wrong.

Just before 5:00 p.m., Maude Rouscher had returned from a house hunting tour with her husband. Police believe that Spangler knew that her troubled marriage was on the mend and that the couple was trying to reconcile.

She had told her parents that Spangler had threatened to kill her and her husband if they ever got back together. "If I can't have you, he can't either," she quoted Spangler as saying. She even told relatives that she was going to see the district attorney about the threats.

Before that could happen, though, Spangler entered the house while everyone was gone and waited in the kitchen, where his jealousy boiled over into rage. On the stove, police found a coffeepot full of hot lye water. They believe that Spangler had intended to scald his victim with the caustic brew but decided instead on a swift murder by hammer and razor blade. Neighbors saw him leave the scene, and the hunt began for Spangler, who had a reputation for chasing after married women.

An advisory over the radio described the fugitive and his clothing. Local police already knew Spangler by sight because of his involvement in the murder of Sarah Meckley back on August 1925. For that crime, Spangler was sentenced in February 1926 to ten to twenty years in state prison but was released in late May 1931. Had word of the threats reached the district attorney, Spangler would have been arrested and put back in jail.

City police found evidence that Spangler had taken an indirect route through the outskirts from School Alley to the brickyard south of Prospect Street. Burrs on his coat and trouser legs indicated that he had crept through weed patches and fields instead of traveling on the road and open ground. He had forced open the office door and had used the shotgun kept there by a coworker.

Years before his suicide, Spangler had a run-in with vigilantes out to teach him a lesson about the evils of adultery. As the story goes, he was having an affair with an Abbottstown woman whose husband had won the sympathy of other ladies. They convinced their male relatives to punish Spangler for his unwelcome visits to their neighborhood. The men stopped the couple on one of their secret liaisons and promptly told them to step out of the buggy. While Spangler was held captive, the woman was told to leave, which she did under protest.

The men unhitched the horse from the buggy, removed its harness and set the animal free. They then cut the harness into pieces, removed the buggy top, detached the wheels from the axles and slashed the upholstery with knives. They rolled the wheels down a hill and overturned the buggy. Meanwhile, Spangler muttered curses under his breath, which later became cries of pain as he was flogged repeatedly by his own whip. The vigilantes then dunked Spangler in a nearby creek and threatened to lynch him should he ever return to Adams County.

Spangler never pressed charges, even though his assailants wore no masks or disguises and were known to him. There was speculation that they may have been members of the Ku Klux Klan and that the woman may have been Sarah Meckley. What is known is that the shooting of the mother of four was the result of two years of growing tensions between Spangler and her husband.

Perhaps the most dramatic incident was when Charles Meckley got word that his wife, Sarah, was seen joyriding in Spangler's car. Armed with a shotgun, he rushed across the Lincoln Highway to confront Spangler after seeing her leave the car parked in front of the family home. Instead of getting out as ordered, Spangler hit the gas and drove toward Charles Meckley, who stepped aside and fired a load of shot into the rear of the car. As a result, Spangler brought charges against the husband for assault.

Before this, in February 1924, Charles Meckley had caught his wife with Spangler and threatened to kill the other man. Charges in this case were settled out of court. The final straw came with the birth of Ervin Meckley about fourteen months before the shooting. Questions over who fathered this child prompted Sarah to leave Charles and live with her sister in Thomasville.

The night of the shooting, Spangler met up with Sarah in downtown York, where they did some window-shopping. He then drove her to Baumgardner's

This vintage postcard of downtown York shows some of the department stores where Sarah Meckley was window-shopping before being mortally shot by Ervin Spangler. *From the collection of the York County Heritage Trust, York, Pennsylvania.*

Woods, a romantic spot southeast of the city. There, an argument ensued, followed by a single gunshot that was heard by Harry Snellbaker, who lived about a block away. As he ran to the scene, a woman screamed, "My God, you've shot me." Snellbaker then saw a couple tussling in a Ford coupe, but the driver sped off before he could come any closer. Snellbaker ran home and called the police. It was about 7:45 p.m.

The couple was next seen on the north side of the 600 block of West College Street. There, local residents heard a woman shout, "Hold him…Don't let him get away," as Sarah Meckley ran from a Ford coupe before collapsing on a plot of grass in front of a vacant lot. Police arrived to find her on the ground. As a detective loaded her into a taxicab, she pointed to Spangler and cried out, "He shot me…He shot me." Police arrested Spangler and took him to city hall, while she was transported to York Hospital and admitted.

Police obtained a sworn statement from Sarah Meckley before she was taken into surgery. In it, she accused Spangler of shooting her in the back as she turned to run into the woods. He picked her up, laid her in the car and asked her to promise not to tell anyone who shot her. "Then he got a razor and was going to cut my throat," Meckley said. "I grabbed the razor and cut my hand." After a struggle, she took it from him and threw it out the car window.

On their ride to York, they were "going like the wind," but Spangler did not know how to find the hospital. Finally, he stopped the car on West College Avenue to ask a passerby for directions. As he did this, Meckley pulled the keys from the ignition, opened the car door and ran out, shouting, "Don't let that man get me!"

Indeed, she had a deep cut on her right palm and a slight laceration on her neck, but the wound that proved fatal was caused by a bullet that had pierced her stomach wall at two places and caused massive internal bleeding. There were beads of sweat on her brow as she talked to police. Her face lacked color. She told officers, "For God's sake. Don't let him go. He'll kill me again."

As doctors tried to save her, Spangler had a visitor. His father, Clayton, arrived at city hall after a reporter told him about the shooting. His only emotion was disgust over what Ervin had done. He explained to reporters how he had warned his son for the past two years to stay away from that woman. "Ever since he became intimate with her, he brought one sorrow after another into the home," the father said.

Clayton built his son a home next door to his, hoping that it would draw his attention away from Meckley. He also bought Ervin a car on the promise

This image shows the women's ward of the old York Hospital, circa 1900. *From the collection of the York County Heritage Trust, York, Pennsylvania.*

that his son would pay him back, but Ervin spent all of his money on clothing for Sarah, and that might have been why she died. Upon her death, police upgraded the initial charge to murder.

At first, Spangler denied even shooting the woman. He claimed that someone unseen had crept up to the car and shot her from ambush. He changed this story into a confession under the pressure of a police interrogation. Spangler told officers that he met Sarah that night on the York Square at about 7:00 p.m. As they window-shopped, she showed him a dress and fur coat that she wanted him to buy, but he told her that he was out of work and could not afford the purchase. She later cursed him out in the woods for not buying the clothes.

Spangler then showed her a document verifying the transfer of fire insurance on the house from his name to his father's name. This only upset her more because she wanted Spangler to sell the house and use the money to buy her gifts. Her plan was to leave her husband and shack up with

Spangler in York so he could take care of her family. She often complained that Charlie treated her wrong.

Spangler claimed that it was Sarah who pulled a razor from her purse and assaulted him. He was able to subdue her, but she jumped out of the car and hollered "Murder" several times before she started to run. That was when Spangler fired the gun once, and she fell to her knees. He placed her in the car and started toward York Hospital.

A jury in February 1926 took about two hours to convict Spangler of second-degree murder. The credibility of the defendant may have been a factor since Spangler had multiple versions of what happened in the car the night of the shooting.

Spangler testified at trial that Sarah Meckley gave him poison to slip into his parents' coffeepot. She wanted his parents dead so he would inherit their property and be able to run away with her. "Do this thing…then we'll have plenty of money," he quoted her as saying. When he refused to follow through on her request, a bitter argument ensued within the car.

Police did find a box of poison under the car seat where Spangler said he put it after receiving it from her just days before. But the prosecution turned this around and asked Spangler, "Didn't you tell Meckley you would furnish the poison to kill her husband." The defense objected saying the question lacked foundation and could prejudice the minds of jurors.

In his confession, Spangler said that he shot Sarah Meckley after she left the car. At trial, he claimed that the gun went off accidentally inside the car after the argument over the house turned violent. On the stand, Spangler testified that Meckley not only pulled a razor from her purse but also the revolver out of some paper wrapping. He claimed that he gave her the handgun some time ago for protection and that she kept it concealed as a package. The night of the shooting, Sarah pulled out the gun and set it beside her as the couple was traveling toward Baumgardner's Woods.

The trouble was that the defense could not produce any forensic evidence proving that the bullet had gone through Meckley and into the car, as it would have if the shooting had taken place inside. An effort by the defense to have letters from Meckley admitted as evidence also failed.

The hope was that the letters would prove a defense theory that she was obsessed over Spangler and had threatened to swear her life on him. Spangler testified how he was with her almost every night and had received many letters asking him for romantic encounters. Spangler had known Sarah Meckley for six years, having met her in Thomasville, where they both lived. He had been her boyfriend for about four years.

PART IV
HELL HATH NO FURY

Murder has always been an equal-opportunity destroyer. His and her crime is a sad fact of life. Feminine wiles can be just as lethal as any dose of masculine violence fueled by testosterone. In the pages that follow, you will meet three women. One is very direct in her need to possess—hitting her man where it hurts the most—while the other two ladies deliver their venom in far more subtle ways. They have in common a deluded sense of what it means to love and what it takes to be faithful in a confusing society dominated by male role models.

"Wickedest Creature": The Confession of Elizabeth Moore

Visions of heaven and hell haunted runaway slave Elizabeth Moore and may have lingered in her mind as regret as she was hanged from the gallows. She blamed her death on the deeds of her masters, claiming that ignorance of faith drove her to murder her own children. But who can tell whether she won salvation even as she warned the rest of us not to stray from the righteous path.

Moore's story began in Havre de Grace, Maryland, where she was born into a family of eight children and sold to William Gibson when she was eight years old. It was understood that Elizabeth would be in his service until age eighteen, but his marriage two years before the end of that term changed the plan, as explained by Moore herself in her confession filed

CONFESSION OF ELIZABETH MOORE,

Together with the Farewell Address of *John Charles*, and the sentence of the court pronounced on them both:—Who were executed at York, (Pa.) the 27th of May, 1809.

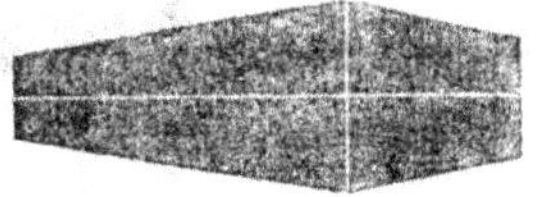

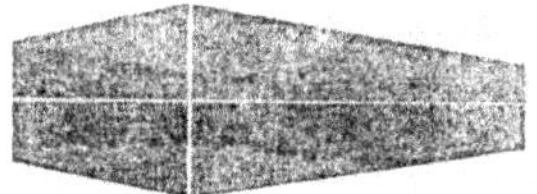

SENTENCE.

AT A COURT OF OYER AND TERMINER held at York, for the county of York—of April term, 1809: ELIZABETH MOORE and JOHN CHARLES were respectively tried;—the former for murdering *Isaac Bateman*, her own child, between two and three years old, by means of poison. The latter for the murder of *Henry Young*, his master, by means of stabbing.

The prisoners were well assisted by counsel assigned by the court, and on full and fair trials (every indulgence being granted to them and their counsel, by the court.) The prisoners were respectively found *Guilty of Murder in the first Degree*, and on the 12th day of April last, were brought together before the court, to receive sentence of death. The court-house was filled with spectators on this awful occasion—and a solemn silence prevailed. The president of the court (*Judge Henry*) asked each of the prisoners, in presence of their counsel, if any reasons were to be assigned, Why Sentence of Death should not be pronounced? None were alledged by either. Upon which his honor addressed both the prisoners in substance as follows:

ELIZABETH MOORE and JOHN CHARLES you have each of you been tried, and found guilty on full and decided proof, of murder of the first degree. The verdicts thus found forfeit your lives, and subject you to the punishment of death. It is often expected by persons in your situation, that the pardoning power will interfere, and that the sentence of the law will thereby be avoided; hopes of this kind, entertained by either of you, will be vain and delusive. The circumstances attending each of your crimes are of so aggrieved a nature, and discover so much depravity of heart, that the governor of the state would never so far risk his reputation, as to exercise mercy in cases so atrocious, and tending by their example to the destruction of society—for if offenders, such as you are, [illegible] society would not long exist. Be advised then to turn your thoughts to another world, the short time that you are allowed to live in this. Although you have no reason to expect pardon from an earthly judge—the mercy of heaven is unbounded. To this source let me advise you to apply with sincere and penitent hearts—although your sins are great, the mercy of God through Christ is greater; for this purpose I would advise you to ask the aid of the clergy, they will point out to you the path of duty, and direct you to the only fountain of comfort and mercy. The painful task remains for me to pronounce the sentence of the law.

ELIZABETH MOORE. It is the sentence of this court, that you be conducted back to the prison from whence you have been taken, and from thence to the place of execution, and that you be there HANGED BY THE NECK, UNTIL YOU ARE DEAD. And you JOHN CHARLES, in like manner—and may *God have Mercy on your Souls.*

CONFESSION.

I WAS born in Havre-de-Grace, in the state of Maryland. My mother was a slave to *Solomon Brown*—I know nothing of my father. I had four brothers and four sisters when I left home. When I was in the eighth year of my age I was sold to one *William Gibson*, of the same place, until I should arrive at eighteen years. Not one of my masters give me any education. William Gibson was an old batchelor,—he got married about two years before I was free. My mistress became so cross to me that I ran away before my time was up, and came to York, in Pennsylvania, where I was taken up for a runaway and confined in gaol. From thence I was discharged by the court. I then hired myself by the month from place to place, for a few years, in which time I became with child by a man of the name of R. B. When my child was a month old, I bound myself to *George Test*, for two years. During this servitude I got with child by one *Gibbon*, a negro—he promised to marry me, but deceived me, as he had another girl. He, Gibbon, first put it into my head that I should try to destroy this child in the womb before it was born. He procured me some stuff for this purpose. I took it, but it had not the desired effect. I then concluded in my mind that I would destroy the child when it would be born. I was delivered of a daughter—By this time my son by B—— was about eighteen months old, and was then taken to the poor-house, at York. I loved Isaac, the eldest; but I did not like my daughter. When it was three days old the Devil put it into my head to smother my daughter in the bed. I turned myself and looked at the child, and then wished I had never seen the little devil, as I called it. With this resolution I took it up in my arms, and smothered it until expired. This is the first crime I brought to maturity. When I lived with Gibson I went one day to gather some dock for greens. I took the broad leafed dock, believing it was poison. My master saw the dock before it was cooked, and scolded me very much, and told me it was poison.

I was eighteen years old before I had any information that there was a future state. I thought when the body was laid in the grave there was an end of it. When I lived at *Test's* I went several times to Methodist meeting, but was so ignorant I did not know the sense of what was said there. I at last got my eyes opened and got understanding—At this time I thought I was the wickedest creature on earth, and was afraid the earth would open and swallow me up. One day as I was walking in the yard there came a voice to me to go to prayer—I looked all around but saw no one. I then went into the house and was perplexed to know where the voice came from. I thought it came from Heaven. I went out the second time and the same voice came the second time *Go on to prayer*. I then went up stairs and went on my knees and prayed—A short time after this I dreamed two dreams, the first whereof is as follows—I saw in my dream two roads, one broad and one narrow—I took the narrow one and went on a little peace, when I came to a spring that was in—I thought it was the water of life—I drank and washed myself in it, and then went a little way further, and saw a very high wall. I made three attempts to get to the top of this—I at last got to the top of it, and sat on the top of the wall and looked all around, and saw a great building. I then saw two gates—I then went towards those gates. I then saw a great company of Angels going in at the gates. I was not there when [illegible] I at last came to the gate—there was two Angels opened the gate—I went in and went forward a little way, when I discovered two other Angels and two other gates—I at last got to the building, when I came to the door and knocked, and the Virgin Mary opened the door, and I went in and saw our Saviour setting on a throne—I saw four lamps burning, one at each side, one behind and one before—I saw a great company of Angels singing and praising God. When they had done singing, the Lord told one of the Angels to shew me what kind of a place everlasting torment was. There was an old man with an iron rake raking people into the place of torment. The Angel told me that the old man was Belzebub. When I saw this place I was much afraid. Then the Angel told me not to be afraid, he dare not touch you. I then turned away and would have fallen in, but the Angel caught me and took me a small distance, and left me. I then got awake and was much afraid—I at this time tried to pray, but could not. I dreamed a second time that the world was at end. I thought the stars were melting like pewter, and the sky was all in blaze, and the earth was rolling round and round—I tho't there was a great river—I saw people run into the river, and heard them say they would be saved—I saw this but was not afraid—I saw a man that was very much afraid, I told him to pray, he answered, it is too late for me to pray. I then got awake and ran to the door, to see if there was any reality in my dream; so much was I disordered by it in my mind after those two dreams, that I was almost distracted. I thought my soul was lost, and had no hopes of mercy. I tried to pray, but received no benefit. At night in my bed, I thought the devil came to me. I went out to the woods several times to hang myself to a sappling with my handkerchief, when I was about to make the attempt, my conscience checked me and told me to pray. I went on my knees and prayed, but received no benefit thereby.

I am now to relate the murder of my son, *Isaac Bateman*, for which I must shortly suffer the punishment due to the worst of crimes. This child I did not kill out of spite; I loved him and killed him to send his soul to heaven. I thought his sister was in heaven, and I wanted him there too. I tho't at this time my own soul was lost, but that I would make sure of the child—that if it died young, it would no doubt go to heaven. I thought on the other hand, if he would grow to be a man, he might take to drinking and other bad crimes, and thereby come to a bad end. I considered what would be the easiest death for him to die—I fixed on poison as the easiest for him. The devil would give me no rest until I would commit this horrid crime. I started from home on Saturday the 22d of April, to procure three cents worth of poison. I went to different shops but got none. I at last got some at Mr. Mundorff's. I stayed in town all night after I procured the poison. Next day being Sunday, I went to Methodist meeting, and prayed to God, if it was wrong for me to give my child poison, that God should check my conscience. I got no check of conscience. When meeting was out, Mrs. Choice, asked me to go home with her to George Test's—I told her I was going out to the poor-house. It was Gods mercy that I did not go home with the woman, for if I had, I would have taken the life of George Test's two children, John and Wensly Test. I once gave those children swamp cabbage tea, with an expectation that it would poison them, but it did not hurt them. I had no spite at them, further, than I thought I would not be troubled with them, as my child had not leave to stay with me there. This is the only time, I ever attempted to hurt any of George Test's family. I then went out to the poor-house, and took my son from his nurse, and went with him to the spring, and gave him a drink of water, and then took him to the necessary. I then went on my knees to pray, that if it was wrong God should check my conscience. I got no check, and then opened the paper and gave my son some in his hand, and said "here Isaac, eat this," he then licked the poison out of the paper. I then turned round and said, "poor little thing, you are here now, but your soul will soon be in heaven." I took the remainder of the poison from the child, and threw it in the necessary. I then took the child under a tree, and stayed there a short time, and then took him to the spring a second time, and gave him a drink of water. I then took him to the house and put him in the cradle. He laid a few minutes in the cradle, and began to vomit. I then took him on my lap, and laid him in the cradle again. He lived about two hours and a [illegible] I was instantly suspected of murdering my child. I was so suspected, that I was committed to gaol, where I now remain under sentence of death.

I became acquainted, while in gaol, with a man of the name of G***** B***** by whom I became pregnant, and was delivered of a daughter while in gaol. This child, I hope will be brought up in the fear of the Lord, and that her father will do something for her is the earnest desire of her condemned mother. I am sorry I ever said any thing against my evidences, and hope they will forgive me. I am thankful to the Rev. *Robert Cathcart* for what instructions he gave me; and to *John Dobbin* and other men and women of the Methodist Society for their instructions to me, and for their christian admonitions in [illegible] Redeemer. I am truly thankful to the gaoler, Robert Wilson and his family, for their kind and humane treatment of me during my whole confinement. I hope that all who may read these lines will take warning by my shameful end, and shun those fatal paths that I have walked in. I hope also that my fatal end may be a warning to all masters and mistresses who have negroes under their care—may timely instruct them in the path of religion, which is their indispensible duty so to do. I hope the Lord has forgiven me, for I committed these crimes through ignorance.

her
ELIZABETH × MOORE.
mark.

In presence of
M. Klinefelter, Esq. High Sheriff, *J. Dobbin, John Forsyth, Esq. and Robert Wilson*, gaoler.

FAREWELL ADDRESS.

I, JOHN CHARLES, do render my thanks to the governor, for giving me time to repent. I have had a fair and impartial trial. I render thanks to all who visited me in my confinement. I have received great kindness and humanity from the gaoler and his family, and hope God will reward them for it. The sheriff has also shewed me kindnesses, for which I heartily thank him. I cannot leave the world without expressing my thankfulness to *Richard Koch, and his family*, for the great kindness they shewed me while in prison. Finally, I bid all my friends adieu. I confess myself guilty of the crime for which I am to suffer, and the justness of the sentence pronounced on me by the court. I hope that the Almighty will forgive me for this, and many other crimes, and that hardened sinners, who are to live after me, will profit by my example. To this world and all that is therein, I bid a long and last adieu. May God have mercy on my soul.

The original post bulletin of the confession of Elizabeth Moore. *From the collection of the York County Heritage Trust, York, Pennsylvania.*

in county court records: "The mistress became so cross to me, I ran away before my time was up. I came to York and was taken up for a runaway and confined in jail. Discharged by the court, I hired myself out by the month from place to place for a number of years."

During this time, she became pregnant by a man known as "R.B." and delivered a son named Isaac Bateman. When he was a month old, Moore bound herself to George Test for two years. During this servitude, she got pregnant again—this time by a black man named Gibbon, who encouraged her to have an abortion and even procured drugs for her to kill the baby in the womb. The drugs did not work, so Elizabeth decided to smother her daughter in her arms three days after it was born. In her confession, Moore claimed that the devil convinced her to commit the crime in bed while she and her daughter were staying at the York poorhouse.

Moore said that she was eighteen when she first learned that there was an afterlife. Before, she thought that the grave was the end of existence. She cast blame in her confession:

> *Not one of my masters gave me an education. When I lived at Tests, I went several times to the Methodist meeting. So ignorant, I did not know what was said there. At last, I got my eyes open and got an understanding. At this time, I thought I was the wickedest creature on earth. I was afraid the earth would open and swallow me up.*

Her newfound faith did little to comfort Moore. Instead, things only got worse. She explained how one day, while walking in the yard, a voice came to her urging her to pray. Moore bowed down on her knees but ended up falling asleep and having two vivid dreams.

In the first dream, she came upon two roads, one broad and one narrow. She took the narrow path and came upon a spring that she thought was the Water of Life. She drank from it and washed before setting out again. Farther on, she came to a wall so high that it took three attempts before she could climb to the top of it. There she sat and looked around the dreamscape.

In the distance, Moore saw a great company of angels march through a set of gates and into a large building. She followed and was let in the door by the Virgin Mary, whose son Jesus sat on a throne in a large chamber attended by angels praising God. When they were done singing, Jesus turned to Moore and ordered the angels to show her a place of everlasting torment. In her dream, she saw Beelzebub as an old man with an iron rake gathering up souls. "When I saw this place, I was much afraid. An angel told me not to be afraid. I turned away and would have fallen in, but an angel caught me, took me a small distance and left me."

Moore awoke, but only briefly, before falling asleep again. "I dreamed a second time the world was at an end. The stars were melting like pewter. The sky was all in blaze. The earth was rolling round and round…I saw people run into the river, and heard them say they would be saved. I saw a man very much afraid. I told him to pray. He answered it is too late for *me* to pray."

The dreams haunted her as a waking nightmare—a distraction she could not escape. Moore thought that her soul was lost and that there was no hope of mercy. Prayer brought her no peace: "At night, the Devil came to me. I went out to the woods several times to hang myself to a sapling with my handkerchief. When I was about to make the attempt, my conscience checked me and told me to pray. I went on my knees and prayed, but received no benefit."

It was at this time that Moore thought of murdering her son. She would confess to a different motive and consider the easiest way for Isaac to die: "This child, I did not kill out of spite; I loved him. I killed him to send his soul to Heaven…His sister was in Heaven. I wanted him there too. I thought my own soul was lost, but that I would make sure of the child. If he would grow up to be a man, he might take to drinking and other bad crimes and come to a bad end. The Devil would give me no rest until I would commit this horrid crime."

So Moore settled on poison, purchasing three pennies worth of toxin on April 23, 1808. The next day, she attended a Methodist meeting and prayed to God that if it was wrong to give her child poison he should check her conscience.

There was no answer. Moore went to the poorhouse and took her son from his nurse. By this time, the child was about two years old. She gave him a drink of water and took him to an outhouse, where she prayed one last time for God to check her conscience. Her confession records what happened next: "I got no check, opened the paper and gave my son some [poison] in his hand and said 'Here Isaac, eat this.' He then licked the poison off the paper. I then turned around and said 'Poor little thing, you are here now, but your soul will soon be in Heaven."

Moore threw the rest of the poison into the toilet and then sat with Isaac under a tree to wait out the end. They stayed there for a short time before Moore took Isaac to a spring a second time and gave him a drink of water. She then took him back home and placed her son in a cradle, where he died almost three hours later. Moore was a suspect immediately.

While in jail on a charge of murder, she became pregnant to a man named "G.B." and delivered a daughter, who survived. "This child I hope will be brought up in the fear of the Lord," Moore said in her confession. "Her father will do something for her. That is my earnest desire."

During the April 1809 term of court, a jury found Moore guilty of first-degree murder, and she was sentenced to death by hanging. President Judge Henry explained to her the futility of seeking a pardon from the death penalty: "Hopes of this kind will be vain and delusive. The circumstances attending your crimes are so aggrieved a nature and discover so much depravity of heart, that the governor…would never…risk his reputation…to exercise mercy."

Instead, he suggested Moore seek advice from a clergyman and "turn your thoughts to another world, the short time…you are allowed to live in this. Although you have no reason to expect a pardon from an earthly judge—the mercy of Heaven is unbounded." Moore was executed in York on May 27, 1809. In her confession, she stated, "I hope the Lord has forgiven me, for I committed those crimes through ignorance. I hope all who read these lines will take warning by my shameful end and shun these fatal paths that I have walked in."

"BLOTTING OUT THE ROSES": THE WINTER OF KATE NESS

Kate Ness must have been a beautiful flower to those who knew her. Petite, jolly and charming, she held young and old in her sway. Her death notice in a Philadelphia newspaper dubbed her "Queen of Jacobus," her hometown. "She was more than the belle of the village. She was its pride…She exerted a gentle, but unwavering thrall," reported the *North American*. But alas, poor Miss Paradise, as she was also known, was destined to suffer an early death at the Eastern State Penitentiary. The cruel irony was that love for one man drove her to commit a botched murder-suicide that left her victim alive but condemned her to a slow form of self-destruction.

It is strange how beauty and charm can stay with a person. Even in prison, Queen Kate held court as friends made her the subject of their increased attentions, the newspaper reported. "Her life in jail…was one of ease and comfort. Men and women came bearing gifts. Her cell was not a cell. It was the apartment of milady." Neither a kind word nor deed could dispel the curse of a poor constitution along with the grim progress of what may have been pneumonia or consumption. The newspaper described how death came to Ness in February 1903, when she was just twenty-three years old: "As the months went by, the fair prisoner pined. The bloom left her cheek. The old laugh was gone from her sweet young face. The brand of prison life was slowly but surely blotting out the roses."

Kate's ordeal began on October 28, 1901, in York city. Patrolman Hilbert was alerted to trouble by the gunshots and arrived to find local contractor Horace Epley hobbling down Queen Street, followed closely by his mistress Kate Ness. She caught up with Epley, and together they made it to Market Street and the office of Dr. Raymond Butz. Epley leaned on his assailant the whole time.

Bursting in, the victim cried out, "I'm shot!" Perplexed, the doctor asked, "Who shot you?" A hysterical Miss Paradise lamented, "I shot him…How could I have done it, Horace! I love the very ground you trod upon." Butz examined the wounds and sent for an ambulance to take Epley to the hospital. Ness jumped right in and sat beside him as further proof that Epley had failed to disentangle himself from the toxic affair and return home to his wife and children.

Dr. Raymond Butz, circa 1900. *From the collection of the York County Heritage Trust, York, Pennsylvania.*

Police investigators learned how Ness had fired four shots at Epley from about a yard away, resulting in three wounds. One bullet was lodged in his groin. Another had entered the groin but had become lodged in his back muscles. The third bullet cut a flesh wound across his abdomen. The bullets missed vital organs, so Epley eventually recovered.

Officers arrested Ness and transported her to county jail. On the way, she reportedly confessed to the crime by saying, "I had planned to kill Horace a month ago, because I thought he was not true to me. I intended to kill him and then shoot myself. I don't want to live without him…so I thought…we could die together." Her only regret was that she didn't succeed.

Police searched the home of Miss Annie Burtner in the first block of South Queen Street, where Ness had been staying for the past six weeks. There investigators found the revolver used in the crime along with a letter dated October 1901 to Albert Ness, the defendant's father:

> *Father and mother, if I dare call you so, I know I have made you the most trouble in the family. I guess what I am about to do will set you crazy, but*

A horse-drawn York city ambulance, circa April 1907. *From the collection of the York County Heritage Trust, York, Pennsylvania.*

> *I am half crazy myself and I don't care to live any longer...Oh, I lived happy for two years, but now I am the most unhappy woman in this world. All for the love of a man, but I am not sorry I met him. He was good and kind to me only that he is married and he brought me to what I am now.*

As in her confession, Ness wrote how she could never give up Epley or live without him. She told her parents how she wished she had never been born to bring a bad name to her family. The prosecution was convinced that enough evidence existed to prove premeditation and their most serious charge of assault with intent to kill. Her trial was held in January 1902.

The notoriety of the victim and suspect drew a packed house to the courtroom of Judge John Bittenger. Every seat was occupied, and spectators not only lined up four deep in the rear of the room but also surged up the side aisles to the jury boxes and out the corridor. It appeared as though the flower of Jacobus was wilting long before her conviction and time spent in state prison. In court, she appeared thin and haggard from three months in county lockup. Her face had a ghostly pallor, one reporter observed. Yet when other women testified against her, Queen Kate would lean forward slightly and take on a look of pure contempt for those who were betraying her.

Witnesses agreed that, shortly after 7:00 p.m., the night of the shooting, Epley called on Ness at the Burtner home. The couple went out into the backyard, where they argued before returning to the house, where the shooting took place at about 7:45 p.m. By then, the other occupants had left.

Lawyers for the defense built their case on a combination of self-defense and, "I didn't know it was loaded." They had a friend in Epley who, at one point, was planning to ask prosecutors to drop charges against his former lover. On the stand, he tried to shield Ness and deflect blame to himself. Epley testified that he had visited Ness that night to talk her out of pursuing a lawsuit against a woman to recover a disputed rocking chair. Ness was ready to go before an alderman to argue her case, but Epley tore her hat to pieces. This angered her, kindling an argument that turned physical when an intoxicated Epley slapped her in the face while they were out in the backyard.

Ness then pulled out the revolver that Epley had let her borrow as protection for when she went out into the countryside. The victim testified that he took the weapon from her, removed the bullets and threw the gun farther into the yard. Epley went away for about ten minutes. He returned to find the empty revolver on the table. Epley said that he then reloaded the gun, unbeknownst to Ness, who was crying in another room.

Their argument flared up again, during which time Epley struck Ness in the face before grabbing her roughly by the shoulders and hitting her again. In the struggle that followed, Queen Kate got hold of the handgun and pulled the trigger. Epley testified that she fired in self-defense and without criminal intent. He claimed that Ness said she didn't know that the pistol was loaded.

On the witness stand, Ness testified that she hid the gun on her person when they went out into the yard. She then corroborated his story of abuse and how he had disposed of the handgun. But Ness said that Epley had left for twenty-five minutes before returning to find her in a chair with her face in her hands. She testified that the argument resumed, along with the abuse Epley mentioned. Ness said that in all of the excitement, she grabbed the revolver and pulled the trigger three times in rapid succession in what she called an "almost involuntary" act goaded on by the indignities inflicted upon her. Ness claimed how before in the backyard, she only pointed the revolver at Epley to frighten him. She denied making any confession to police except to say that she was sorry that she had shot Epley. She further denied making any threats against her lover except in a joking manner.

Meanwhile, the prosecution tried to prove that Ness had planned the shooting in advance. Annie Burtner testified how she overheard Epley tell Ness, "I am done with you, now and forever. I am going back to my family." The prosecution claimed that it was Ness who disappeared long enough to retrieve and reload the revolver. The theory was that Ness had shot Epley as the victim was turning to open the front door after he told her goodbye forever. The first shot entered his groin and penetrated about four inches. As he turned around, Epley asked her what was the matter, and Ness fired the second bullet, which grazed his side. The third shot missed, but the fourth bullet hit Epley.

Judge Bittenger believed that Ness had every intention to carry out her murder-suicide plot but that her nerve failed her and her affection for Epley returned. This conclusion is supported by testimony that Ness had followed Epley out the door, begging him to return and rest on a lounge while she called a doctor. The prosecution believed that it was Epley who had snatched away the handgun and put it on a bureau as he was leaving to get help.

Defense attorneys asked the court to instruct the jury to acquit Ness on the charge of assault with intent to kill, stating that the evidence proved that it was a crime of passion, not premeditation. Jurors deliberated for just over two hours before convicting Ness of aggravated assault but finding her not guilty of the more serious charge. She pled guilty to carrying a concealed weapon.

This verdict upset the judge, who thought that the evidence was clear and convincing that Ness had intended to kill both herself and Epley. Bittenger added that the facts warranted the maximum penalty of two years and nine months of hard labor and solitary confinement at a state prison on the assault conviction. As for the weapons charge, he sentenced her to an additional year. Ness would only survive little more than twelve months before returning to Jacobus in a coffin. The same day he sentenced Ness to prison, Bittenger issued a warning to Epley not to abuse his wife or fail to support this family again or he would come up on charges. Local newspapers had reported how Epley had returned to his family only to assault his wife while intoxicated. Horace Epley would die twenty-eight years later in 1930.

"By Criminal Intimacy": The Black Widow Love Triangle

The agony must have been unbearable for Joshua Tracey. Convulsions seized his body, causing so much pain that his fingernails tore at the flesh of his chest and feet. His writhing midsection formed an arch supported mostly by his heels, shoulders and the back of his head. It took three to four people just to hold Tracey down—first on the kitchen floor and then on a couch of his Chanceford Township home. Death by strychnine poison was such a bittersweet torture for this farmhand about to meet the Reaper. The date was June 14, 1909.

Neighbor Annie Miller would later testify how she had arrived at the Tracey home shortly after supper the evening Joshua died. "I asked him what was wrong," she recalled. "He said, 'I don't know…heart trouble.' He told me his breast hurt him." Miller then asked Minnie Tracey what was wrong with her husband. The wife told the neighbor that Joshua had drank some whiskey that afternoon and was probably just drunk. Minnie added that twenty-three morphine tablets were also missing.

Dr. David Posey, the attending physician, also asked Joshua what was wrong. "Heart trouble, don't you think Doc?" came the anguished reply, followed by confirmation that the only thing he had taken was the whiskey. Joshua could not have known that he had been poisoned as a result of a conspiracy of his cheating wife and scheming brother-in-law, William R. Brown.

Miller would tell jurors that she overheard Joshua ask his wife, "Min, get your turns down and stand by me. I won't be here long." To which, Minnie answered, "My God, I can't be here and there and everywhere at once!"

before leaving the room. Minnie Tracey stayed away for the thirty to forty-five minutes it took for her husband to die in agony. During his ordeal, Miller talked to Joshua, who at one point apologized for misidentifying the neighbor while he was in the throes of a particularly painful spasm. "Don't blame me for lying," Joshua said. "I can't see; I thought it was Minnie's voice."

Minutes later, Joshua was gone, but before he died Miller went to the kitchen, where she found Minnie Tracey looking out the window. When Miller told Minnie that Joshua was dying, the wife had just one word: "Oh." After he died, Miller returned to the kitchen to tell the widow the news. "She followed me into the room and began to cry," Miller told jurors. "After he was dead, while standing out on the porch, Mrs. Tracey said to me 'I wonder what he died with…I wonder if it was the cramps; he always said it would kill him.'"

When Miller responded that his death was from a "broken heart," Minnie Tracey replied, "Joshua never had any trouble," but that was not what Miller had meant. She knew of the fights that Minnie had with her husband and that Minnie was having an affair with Brown. It was only a matter of time before jurors knew that, too, and they would convict both Minnie Tracey and William Brown in the murder.

At first, Dr. Posey thought that the violent muscle contractions were caused by tetanus, so he asked Joshua whether he had hurt himself while working. The answer was no. The doctor dismissed this theory after finding no injuries on his patient. Convinced that the symptoms matched strychnine poisoning, Posey tried to stop the convulsions by injecting Joshua with morphine, but the treatments didn't work.

His diagnosis, combined with rumors of an affair, prompted the autopsy and subsequent murder investigation. The coroner's inquest found that Joshua had died from asphyxiation brought on by the convulsions. A chemical analysis of his stomach contents confirmed that the fifty-one-year-old victim had ingested a lethal dose of poison. How the toxin got into his system and who was responsible became the focus of the murder trials.

Five minutes before he collapsed and went into convulsions, Joshua was drinking whiskey poured by Minnie from a bottle that they kept in a cupboard. The whiskey had been mixed with coffee from a pot on the stove. He was relaxing after dinner following a day in the fields. Witnesses saw Minnie rinse out the whiskey bottle before returning it back to the cupboard. The old coffeepot was replaced before it could be tested for trace evidence.

Sources described Joshua Tracey as a thrifty worker and devoted father of six children who had been drinking heavily of late due to troubles he had with his thirty-eight-year-old wife. Tensions began after Brown's wife (Joshua's sister) died on March 18, 1908, and Brown and his children became guests of the Tracey household. Soon after moving in, Brown's oldest daughter took sick and died. This fueled speculation after Brown's arrest for Joshua's murder that his wife and daughter had been poisoned and that maybe their bodies should be exhumed to verify the cause of death. That rumor died down, and there was no further mention of these suspicions in newspaper reports.

Brown stayed with the Tracey family until about January or February 1909, when he left. There was conflicting testimony on the reasons for his departure. Brown said that it had nothing to do with adultery, while Minnie testified that it was her idea to purge the household of a source of tension. She and Joshua often argued over the alleged affair. The prosecution theorized that Joshua, fed up by the situation, pushed Minnie to have Brown leave. Regardless, Minnie left Joshua soon after Brown departed, only to return later to her husband.

Neighbors were eager to help police secure as much evidence as possible against Brown and Minnie Tracey. They disliked Brown for his freewheeling lifestyle and the way he made himself virtual master of the Tracey household. There was even speculation that the Ku Klux Klan had threatened Brown to cease his attentions toward Minnie or face the consequences.

Ella Mitzel narrowly cheated death the day of the murder. A houseguest, she had put the glass of whiskey to her lips after Joshua had insisted that she sample it. He had noticed how the whiskey was darker than normal, probably from it being mixed with coffee. Instead of drinking from the glass, Mitzel handed it back to Minnie, saying that the whiskey tasted bitter, like quinine. Later, she would testify how Minnie handed the glass to Joshua, who drained it.

Minnie had confided in Mitzel numerous times about her infidelity with Brown and how she loved him better than any other man. Mitzel testified how she once had caught the couple sitting on the couch in each other's arms, kissing and hugging. Prosecutors believed that Joshua hastened his own death when he caught his wife with Brown in the woods near their home. The husband had threatened to have them both arrested—to which Brown reportedly said that he would fix Joshua. As further proof, the commonwealth entered into evidence a letter that Minnie had written to her father, seeking his advice on how to get a divorce while expressing her admiration for Brown.

That was not all. The prosecution submitted into evidence about fifty letters and postcards that the couple had exchanged in the months leading

The old York County Prison. *Photo by Joseph Cress.*

up to the murder and even after they were arrested and remanded to York County Prison. In some cases, Brown signed his love notes with the code "23-18-2," representing the order his initials appear in the alphabet. One of his cards read: "Remember me the many miles apart and bear in mind that my love shall be yours. I hope to see your sweet face soon and have a kiss from your sweet lips."

In a letter to Brown, Minnie tried her hand at poetry with the following declaration of love:

Remember well and bear in mind,
A true friend is hard to find,
But when you find one that is true,
Pray stick to him as tight as glue.
From your dearest one

Minnie testified in her own defense during her October 1909 murder trial. She told jurors that although she used a powder to spike Joshua's whiskey, she didn't know it was strychnine. Minnie said that Brown had given her the powder on June 12, 1909, claiming that it was a love potion from a powwow doctor that would make her husband care for her more. "He said it would fix him all right and make him treat me better," she quoted Brown before asking jurors, "Why would I've wanted to put an honest, hardworking man out of the way to get one that was no account at all?"

Minnie testified that after dinner on June 14, her husband had several drinks as he fussed over catching her and Brown in the woods together. "He cursed me and called me bad names," she said. "He raised his hand and said if I didn't shut up, he would slap me and kick me out of the house."

Later, as Joshua talked to Mitzel, Minnie went to the cupboard and removed the package that Brown had given her. She then poured the powder into the whiskey bottle in plain view of both of them. When Joshua asked for the last drink in the bottle, she hesitated at first, telling him that he had enough already, but her husband insisted. It was Joshua who had ordered Minnie to rinse out the bottle, which she did using coffee because there was no water in the house. She told jurors that on June 16, Brown came to her home after the funeral. Here is her testimony:

> *He asked me if I had given my husband that stuff he had given me…I said I had…he told me not to tell anybody he had given me anything or he told me to give it to my husband. I said "What in the name of God was in that package that you gave me?" He didn't tell me then, and he hasn't told me to this day. All he said was "Don't worry, I'll take all this on myself."*

This testimony conflicted with the written confession that she gave police soon after her arrest. In that, Minnie claimed that she saw Brown enter the kitchen while her husband was outside working. She told police that Brown had slipped something into the coffeepot from a paper bearing the skull and crossbones. He then gave her instructions to spike the whiskey with strychnine by using the coffee to conceal any color change and suspicious taste.

The jury deliberated for about fourteen hours before finding Minnie Tracey guilty of voluntary manslaughter. The verdict surprised court watchers, who expected nothing less than a second-degree murder conviction. Judge John Bittenger called it a miscarriage of justice, saying that the evidence supported a first-degree murder conviction. "How the jury found such a verdict…is beyond my comprehension," he said.

Minnie seemed relieved at not having to suffer the death penalty or life imprisonment. Instead, she was sentenced to three to twelve years of solitary confinement at the Eastern State Penitentiary. This was the maximum

Judge John Bittenger. *From the collection of the York County Heritage Trust, York, Pennsylvania.*

penalty for voluntary manslaughter. The judge also ordered Minnie confined until she was able to furnish a $2,000 bond for her release, even if that time exceeded the maximum sentence.

The prosecution would later call Minnie as a witness in the January 1910 trial of William Brown. On the stand, she testified that if she had wanted poison to kill rats, she could have bought it herself while she was in York with Joshua just days before the murder. Her statement ran contrary to testimony by Brown that he thought that she had wanted the poison to kill rats, not her husband.

Testifying in his own defense, Brown denied having an affair with Minnie and giving her poison with instructions to administer it as a love potion. He also denied saying anything about taking the blame or suggesting to Minnie that they kill her husband so they could live together. "I never put poison in his coffee pot," Brown told jurors.

It took jurors eighteen hours and as many ballots to convict Brown of second-degree murder. The closest the jury came to the more serious charge was when five jurors voted for first-degree murder while seven voted for second-degree. In reaction to the verdict, Bittenger theorized that the contrary statement by Minnie Tracey cast her in a negative light but spared Brown from the gallows. "She had no motive to perjure her soul to secure your execution," the judge said. "She loved you better than her husband."

Bittenger would later sentence Brown to five to twenty years of solitary confinement and hard labor at Eastern State. At sentencing, the judge reviewed how Brown, having lost his wife, was accepted into the home of his brother-in-law only to have an affair with Minnie Tracey. He had choice words for the defendant: "You found for…yourself a home which, by criminal intimacy, you dishonored and destroyed. Thus you pursued this sinful life."

PART V
BRUTAL HARVEST

If left to ripen on the vine, murder can bear the bitter fruit of freshly planted corpses sunk down in rows. Who can say what crops may grow from seeds of fear, paranoia and depression. Each story that follows took root on a farm before it blossomed into something terrible. We begin with a plot to weed out a hex before turning to the cop killer who plowed on past justice only to dig himself a deeper hole. We end with perhaps the most horrific tale of all—the wholesale slaughter of an entire family at the hands of a Grim Reaper dressed in bloody overalls.

"Lunatic Fringe": The Hex Murder

The snaggle-toothed crone became suspicious of her houseguests. Her dark, shiny eyes began to narrow at their persistent questions about the powwow doctor. Emma Knopp became more guarded in her answers after reporters, posing as friends of the accused, told her that John Blymyer had been charged with the murder of Nelson Rehmeyer. "You can't fool me," the Marietta witch suddenly declared. "I know the police sent you." Despite reassurances, she began to deny earlier statements confirming that Blymyer had told her of the plight of the Milton Hess family. Her advice was for him to bring the family to her—not to bludgeon a man to death and burn the body.

At trial weeks later, Blymyer was firm in his resolve. The thirty-two-year-old drifter testified that he would kill anyone who hexed him—even the judge and attorneys in the courtroom. Before murdering the North

Hopewell Township farmer, Blymyer could not eat or sleep. He felt himself slowly wasting away. The night of the slaying, he slept just fine and had soon regained his peace of mind. Thus Blymyer didn't think it was wrong to kill the hermit. The whole time on the witness stand, this pale, slender man spoke in a tone devoid of emotion as he described the circumstances leading up to the November 27, 1928 murder.

Before Knopp, Blymyer had visited fellow powwow doctors to inquire about the source of the hex placed on him. They thought that Rehmeyer was responsible. When Blymyer visited Knopp to verify his suspicions, the old witch instructed him to stare at a dollar bill she had placed in his palm. To his eyes, the portrait of George Washington faded away and was replaced by the baneful stare of his enemy. Knopp also confirmed that Rehmeyer had cursed the Hess family along with John Curry, a friend of Blymyer's. "She said I would have to get the book 'The Long Lost Friend' or a lock from his head," the defendant testified. To break the curse on them all, Blymyer only needed to burn the book or bury the hair eight feet underground.

For generations, the countryside of York County has been home to a latter-day form of witchcraft called hexerai. Chief among its sacred texts was *The Long Lost Friend*, a Pennsylvania Dutch handbook of spells. In his article "The Witchcraft Murder," writer Roger Butterfield called Rehmeyer "a known student of black magic." He wrote how neighbors tried to avoid passing his house at night, but when they had to, they supposedly muttered passages from the Bible or other books of incantations. Butterfield reported how a faint light was often seen from the kitchen window gleaming late into the night, especially when lightning raked the sky.

It is unknown how much of this was Butterfield being creative, but Jeannette Shank Harvey, a retired teacher, told the *York Daily Record* in 2007 that her mother used to pal around with Nelson Rehmeyer when they were children. Harvey described the victim as a self-educated man and a good person to talk with. Also in 2007, Rickie Ebaugh called his great-grandfather Nelson a faith healer and a well-respected farmer. The investigation of the Hex Murder began with the braying of a mule on Thanksgiving morning, November 29, 1928.

Oscar Glatfelter was traveling down the road when he heard the hungry animal cry out from the stable. He had not seen his neighbor, Nelson Rehmeyer, for days. Glatfelter went to the farmhouse, found the door shut but unlocked and then entered. There he found the charred body facedown on the kitchen floor, covered in blood and the ashes of a mattress and old blanket. An empty coal oil lamp was found next to the body, along with

The WITCHCRAFT MURDER

By
ROGER BUTTERFIELD

Nelson Rehmeyer Was a Hermit of the Hills Who Practiced "Black Magic." But His Art Could Not Save Him, When in His Lonely Cabin He Was Set Upon by the Sinister Visitors Who Sought to Clip His "Witchlock" and Shear Him of His Power. Failing, They Brutally Beat Him to Death, Perpetrating One of Pennsylvania's Strangest Murders.

FAR back among the hills of York county, in rural Pennsylvania, are the lonely, pine-covered slopes of Rehmeyer Valley.

It is the traditional home of a strange and silent race of men—somber, bitterly defiant of modern innovations, and believers in a weird, latter-day form of witchcraft which they call "hexerai."

For more than a century occult practices and black magic have flourished in this isolated section. Witch-doctors, or "hex" doctors, as they are called, minister to the occupants of the old stone farmhouse dotting the countryside, just as medieval soothsayers and magicians ministered to the inhabitants of the Black Forest.

Few people outside of York and the surrounding counties realized the power which these ancient superstitions held over the inhabitants until recently, when a strange and terrible murder suddenly revealed their strength. It was a crime of violence and black art, fire and death, which shook the entire countryside and aroused the nation. The story of what happened reads like some gruesome memoir of the Middle Ages, yet it

Cover page of the "Witchcraft Murder" article by Roger Butterfield as it appeared in the April 1931 edition of the *Illustrated Detective Magazine. From the collection of the York County Heritage Trust, York, Pennsylvania.*

pieces of wood and bloodstained fragments of a broken chair. A hole about a foot and a half in diameter had been burned into the floor, and a knee charred down to the bone had slipped into the opening. Ropes pinned the victim's arms and legs.

Faced at first with a mystery, investigators caught a break while questioning the victim's wife, who lived a mile south of the crime scene. The couple had separated years before but had remained good friends. Mrs. Rehmeyer told police that two men had visited her the night before the murder asking for the whereabouts of her husband. She identified Blymyer as one of the men. He was promptly arrested, along with fourteen-year-old John Curry. The suspects confessed, implicating eighteen-year-old Wilbert Hess in the conspiracy. With evidence in hand, District Attorney Amos Herrmann vowed swift justice. Back-to-back trials were held in January 1929, starting with Blymyer.

The Rehmeyer House, as it appears today in North Hopewell Township. *Photo by Joseph Cress.*

While individual accounts vary, the basic story is that the trio arrived at the victim's home at about 9:30 p.m. on November 27 to obtain either a lock of hair or the spell book from Rehmeyer, who resisted. In the course of subduing the farmer, the trio used firewood and a chair to beat Rehmeyer into submission before tying him up. Sometime during the struggle, the victim died, and a decision was made to conceal the crime through arson.

Herrmann prosecuted each case as a robbery gone bad. While journalists worldwide flocked to York for the first witch trial since Salem, Herrmann carefully avoided any mention of witchcraft or powwowing in his voir dire of jurors and his opening statement in the Blymyer case. The first mention of the supernatural came when Clayton Hess, Wilbert's brother, testified that after killing the victim, Blymyer admitted, "I got the witch." It was Clayton who drove the trio to the woods about a mile from the crime scene the night of the murder. He played no further part.

Originally, Blymyer wanted Clayton to go along on the mission to remove the family curse, but the parents sent Wilbert instead. Already a powwow doctor, Blymyer had met Curry in the cigar factory where they worked. The two became friends, with Blymyer taking the lead as master and Curry as his apprentice. Together, they learned that a recent spell of misfortune had befallen the property and persons of the Milton Hess family of York

Township. There were reports that the crops had failed and the family had lost some chickens. A prize cow no longer gave milk, and several children had taken sick. Milton blamed his sister-in-law, Ida Hess, claiming that she had someone hex the family out of spite following a dispute over a road bordering their properties. It was a charge that she vehemently denied.

Operating under the aliases John Albright and John Russell, Blymyer and Curry exploited the family's faith in powwow doctors by convincing them that the only way they can be free of the hex was if they helped take down Rehmeyer, its alleged source. However, Herrmann argued that witchcraft was just an excuse for robbery—the real motive behind the crime. He noted that instead of cutting hair from the victim's head, the suspects searched the premises for money, and both Blymyer and Curry were wearing gloves that night to avoid leaving fingerprints.

Defense attorney Herbert Cohen argued the insanity defense, claiming that Blymyer had been exposed to notions of witchcraft and powwowing from the time he was eight years old. This so twisted his mind that it put Blymyer in constant fear of being hexed. Myrtle Downing testified that while a boarder at her home Blymyer would lock himself in his room, talk to himself and complain about being bewitched. Experts described him as being insane, feebleminded or suffering from a borderline case of psychoneurosis. The Associated Press reported how Blymyer once escaped from the state hospital in Harrisburg during a baseball game. Judge Ray Sherwood had these words for jurors: "For insanity to be a cause for acquittal, it must be so deeply rooted as to utterly destroy conceptions of right and wrong. It must so control his will to make crime a duty of overwhelming necessity."

It took the jury only ninety minutes to convict Blymyer of first-degree murder and recommend a life sentence. Released in 1953, Blymyer moved

This image shows Detective Charles White, along with Hex Murder suspects John Curry, John Blymyer and Wilbert Hess. It was also published in the *Illustrated Detective Magazine*, dated April 1931. *From the collection of the York County Heritage Trust, York, Pennsylvania.*

to Philadelphia, where he worked as an apartment house manager until his death in 1977.

Curry was next to go to trial. His attorney, Walter van Baman, asked jurors to consider manslaughter instead of first-degree murder. Teary-eyed, Curry testified that he was mistreated at home by an unkind stepfather, who once got arrested by the city truant officer for Curry's repeated absences from school. Unusually tall and stocky, Curry had once enlisted in the army, giving his age as eighteen, before the military issued him a dishonorable discharge. Herrmann asked jurors to disregard the defendant's age and instead base their verdict only on the evidence. He argued that Curry had admitted to pouring oil over the victim's body so that Blymyer could set fire to the corpse. Curry had also admitted to taking money from Rehmeyer while the victim was on his knees begging for his life.

It took jurors just under two hours to convict Curry of first-degree murder and recommend life in prison. Curry served ten years before reenlisting in the army, where he drafted the Normandy invasion maps while serving as a cartographer for General Dwight Eisenhower. A skilled artist, he also designed the shoulder patch for D-Day. He later returned home to Thomasville and died at age forty-nine.

During the third trial, defense attorney Harvey Gross argued that his client, Wilbert Hess, was duped into this crime by the codefendants, who manipulated the family's belief in powwowing. Herrmann countered by saying that Hess had enough hatred to use a piece of wood to administer the fatal blow that fractured Rehmeyer's skull. Hess testified that it was Blymyer who took the wood from him to strike the fatal blow. The third panel of jurors found Hess guilty of second-degree murder, which called for ten to twenty years in prison. Upon parole, Hess returned to his family in Leader Heights and worked as an electroplater until retirement in 1970. He died in 1978 at age sixty-eight.

Records show that Blymyer was admitted to the county home in 1924 for "entertaining a witchcraft delusion." Oscar Altland, superintendent of the home, testified that witchcraft is "one of the...worst forms of delusions" and "one of the hardest to banish from an unbalanced mind." In his opinion, the court should authorize the county to round up individuals similar to Blymyer: "They should be placed in institutions and kept there for life for the safety of society. The believer in witchcraft very often is prone to... violence...[T]hey must be carefully watched."

Similar calls for action echoed through the state. In Philadelphia, Mrs. W. Ellis Groben, speaking before a local women's club, introduced a resolution declaring powwowing a moneymaking scheme involving a "depraved lot of people preying upon a subnormal following." She demanded an immediate investigation to stamp out such practices.

As secretary of the York Medical Society, Dr. P.A. Noll recommended appointing a committee to educate residents on the evils of witchcraft. He envisioned a campaign in which qualified speakers would address public meetings and brochures warning of the danger would be distributed in local waiting rooms. Society members also agreed to lobby state government to add teeth to laws that champion an end to quackery.

The Pennsylvania Health Department conducted its own probe in which Colonel James Duffy, chief of the bureau of field inspections, reviewed death records from the two years before the Hex Murder. County Coroner L.U. Zech identified a handful of cases, mostly of children, in which quackery was suspected. None of these cases involved violence. Instead, it appeared as though loved ones had put too much faith in powwow doctors to treat common ailments instead of seeking out timely medical care from qualified, licensed professionals. At a so-called witchcraft conference,

This drawing of a powwow doctor was done by David Heckert, whose unsolved murder is profiled in this book. *From the collection of the York County Heritage Trust, York, Pennsylvania.*

Duffy denounced powwow doctors as scam artists who preyed on the innocent by holding out the promise that they could cure illness through some occult power.

Fascination over the Hex Murder has endured to the present day. On January 2, 1988, the Strand Capitol Theater in downtown York hosted the world premiere of *Apprentice to Murder*, a film based on the 1928 homicide. The scene had all the glamour of a Hollywood film debut, with moviegoers dressed in evening finery arriving by stretch limousines amid spotlights and theme music blaring from speakers. The nonprofit arts center earned an estimated $22,000 from five sold-out screenings attended by about four thousand people.

York native Howard Grossman produced the movie, which starred Donald Sutherland and told the tragic story of a man caught up in the world of powwowing. Grossman changed the names and only referred to "Pennsylvania" as the setting. He first got the idea as a high school student back in the late 1960s. Over the years, he had researched the case extensively—reading all of the media accounts and court transcripts. He

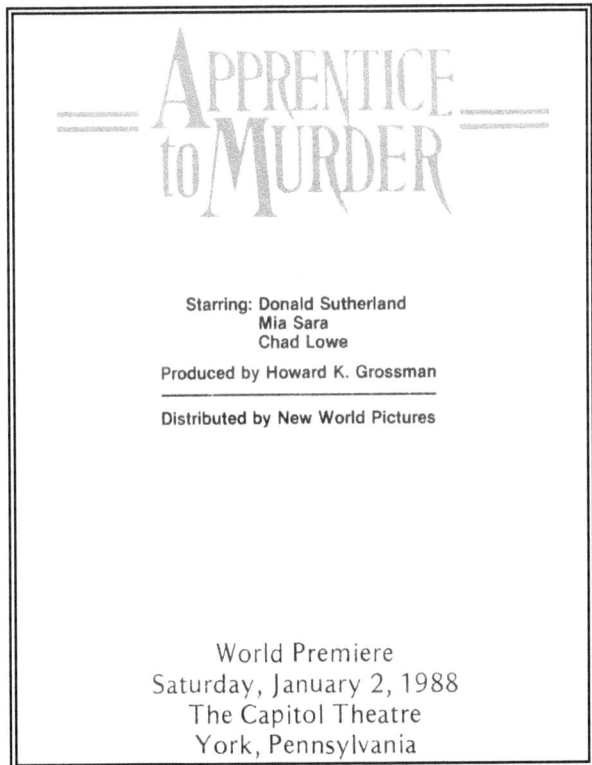

APPRENTICE to MURDER

Starring: Donald Sutherland
Mia Sara
Chad Lowe

Produced by Howard K. Grossman

Distributed by New World Pictures

World Premiere
Saturday, January 2, 1988
The Capitol Theatre
York, Pennsylvania

Souvenir brochure of the *Apprentice to Murder* world premiere. *From the collection of the York County Heritage Trust, York, Pennsylvania.*

took photos of the house and the surrounding landscape. Friends and family backed his project with $200,000 in seed money, which Grossman used to gain the support of investors from Norway, where the film was shot.

A more recent project drew less support and was ultimately abandoned. Since the murder, the Hex House has remained in the Rehmeyer family. In June 2007, Rickie Ebaugh, great-grandson of Nelson Rehmeyer, announced plans to open the house to tours to educate the public on the high-profile murder case and the folk tradition of powwowing.

Ebaugh had partnered with Jerry Duncan, owner of Duncan Media Productions, on a proposal to restore the property to the way it appeared in 1928. This included preserving the burn spot on the floor where the body was found and stocking the interior with original furniture that the family had kept in storage. The men even launched a website on which they defined powwowing as a blend of Pennsylvania Dutch folk medicine and Native American knowledge.

However, they promoted the attraction before obtaining approval from North Hopewell Township. The zoning officer denied their application for a permit on the grounds that it lacked the necessary plan drawings and that the house was not Ebaugh's primary residence. The partners decided not to seek zoning relief, convinced that township officials had already decided to block the project and that a legal battle would prove expensive and fruitless. In an August 2007 editorial, the *York Daily Record* noted that a well-crafted museum could have heightened interest in local history and shed insight into a unique element of the past: "Township reasons for rejecting the plan seemed awfully persnickety. One gets the feeling folks just didn't want a freak show horror attraction in their community."

This was not the first time that officials took issue with the spin of the Hex Murder. Media coverage of the 1929 trials led to articles that cast York County as a backward community of suspicious residents. A *Time* magazine write-up prompted E.A. Hirschman, executive secretary of the York Chamber of Commerce, to write a letter to the editor. In it, Hirschman quoted an excerpt that reported how black cats were allegedly rare in York County because one way of appeasing the devil is to "plop one alive into boiling water and keep the last bone for an amulet."

Hirschman also quoted the article as saying that it was common to see men in York city gather up their hair clippings from the barbershop into paper bags to take home. "If the hair was swept out and birds should build a nest with even one strand of it, the head would ache until the nest was beaten down by the weather," he quoted the article as noting. His letter denied such superstitions: "Every population we know has its lunatic fringe. The nation seems to have discovered it in York County. We treat it only as a fringe and not as the general disease of our politic."

"No Use Hiding": The Death of Officer Sowers

It was pitch black the night Curtis Sowers died, struck down suddenly by a shotgun blast while helping other officers serve an arrest warrant on cattle thieves. Brothers Jacob and William Troup were wanted on charges of larceny and receiving stolen goods after the illegal sale of two calves taken from a farm near Yocumtown. A motorcycle cop from North York, Sowers was asked to assist officer Raymond Bentzel along with constables B.F. Emenheiser and Caleb Altland. What should have been routine was anything but after a single shot echoed throughout the countryside near Bald Hill in Newberry Township. It was May 21, 1929.

To achieve surprise, the officers had parked their vehicle just over a mile from the farmhouse owned by Samuel Troup, the father. They made their way overland and decided to split into two groups to approach the building. Sowers and Bentzel took the back door, while Emenheiser and Altland covered the front door. "We saw one door leading into the house," Bentzel would later testify. "A window close to it had nearly all the panes knocked out. We went on the porch. [Curt] then rapped on the door and said 'When he comes out, I'll get him.' No one came to answer the knock." Sowers then heard a noise from inside the house and yelled "Come out, there's no use hiding."

As Bentzel walked away from the back door and down off the porch, he heard a shot from either the door or an empty window pane. He ran around to the side of the house and saw Sowers lying there. Bentzel did not know if he had been hit or was just playing possum. He waited for only a short time before seeing two figures run away from the house and over a hill. Bentzel went after them, only to find out that they were Emenheiser and Altland. They had interpreted the gunshot as a warning from Sowers that one of the brothers was getting away. Altland would later testify how he had knocked on the front door only to be let in by a stepsister of Jacob Troup. As Altland entered the house, he saw the alleged cattle thief hurry through a door to another room. Altland then heard a single gunshot, which he assumed was Sowers firing at the fleeing Jacob Troup.

What happened next was confusion during a night so dark Emenheiser could not locate Sowers during a sweep of the property, even though he had passed within several feet of the body. This same constable blew his police whistle repeatedly but got no response from the missing police officer. As Emenheiser chased after a shadow, he got jumped by a dog and fell down an incline, losing his gun in the process. That was not all. The surviving officers had no luck finding their vehicle in the pitch black and wandered the hills before being picked up by a local farmer, who drove them to the Lewisberry Inn, where they called the state police shortly after 10:00 p.m.

The survivors returned to find thirty-three-year-old Sowers dead with a blackjack in his left hand and a revolver in his right hand. The World War I veteran left behind a wife named Viola. An autopsy later determined that a shotgun blast from two to four feet away hit Sowers in the face just below the left eye. The shot completely destroyed the posterior nasal cavity, fractured the base of the skull and severed the spinal cord. Death was immediate. Thousands attended the funeral of Sowers, whose body was escorted to burial by a formation of motorcycle cops. In his eulogy, Reverend Harry W. Zuse had this to say: "Life is like a story. The good story is long remembered by the impression it makes upon our hearts while bad…tales are tossed with but little afterthought…Among these good stories, there is one which tears at our minds with anxiety…and fills us with remorse at its ending. It is tragedy."

The Sowers gravestone. *Photo by Joseph Cress.*

The night of the murder, authorities launched one of the most extensive manhunts in York County history. Over the next five days, more than one hundred officers searched for Jacob Troup in the hills and woodlands surrounding his home. To prevent his escape, police sealed off an area within a fifteen-mile radius of the Troup farm and posted guards at every road leading to and from the crime scene. They called in extra manpower from nearby counties to check out every possible hiding place. They were helped by volunteers familiar with the wilderness. At one point, police thought that Troup would make for railroad tracks only miles away to hop a southbound freight train to Virginia, which he had visited only days before the murder. The train would have to slow down to round curves on either side of a bridge, giving Troup the chance to board in relative safety. Nothing ever came of that lead.

There were sightings, along with fear, throughout the county. A woman in Pigeon Hills locked herself in her home after observing a man who matched Troup's description. Another caller told police that he saw a stranger walking along a road carrying a shotgun. As reports came in, search teams were dispatched, but always without results. Either people were mistaken or the fugitive managed somehow to evade the manhunt.

One intriguing report came from a group of men playing cards at a restaurant in Mount Wolf the night of the shooting before word of the murder had reached that town. They told police that a man they recognized as Troup had walked into the restaurant and bought candy at the sales counter. Described as nervous, he was dressed in greasy overalls. When a card player greeted the man by name and asked, "What are you doing here this late at night?" the man replied, "I had a breakdown." He then left. Police thought that the card players were mistaken. There was no way that their prime suspect could have traveled by foot from the Troup farm in Newberry Township to Mount Wolf in just over two hours, but the men at the restaurant were convinced that the fugitive had a ride into town.

One afternoon, a state trooper spotted Troup on a hillside watching his search party. As the trooper kept vigil, a second group of officers closed to within revolver range but was cheated when Troup saw them and fled farther into the hills. Once again, an extensive search turned up nothing. Cut off from food, Troup lived off the land for five days before surrendering to police on May 26. He told arresting officers that the combination of starvation, lack of sleep and fear of vigilante justice prompted him to give up. "He knew he had a chance with the police," the *York Gazette and Daily* reported. "They would not shoot unless he resisted, but the irate farmers might lynch him."

The former fugitive had reason to fear most everyone involved in the manhunt. While in custody, Troup told police that he had nothing to eat for two days when desperation drove him to a farmhouse. As he peeked out from behind a pine tree, Troup saw some state troopers approach. One of them fired a gun, narrowly missing the fugitive, who fled across Beaver Creek and spent the night hunkered down under some driftwood. The next morning, Troup crossed Conewago Creek and spent much of Wednesday and Thursday sleeping out in the woods and on corn sheaves on the mountain. Thursday night, he met up with his brother, William, on a public road and asked for food, which was taken to him.

On Friday, Troup was on Huff's Hill when he saw two men on the slope above him. One of them hollered words that Troup could not understand, but there was no misunderstanding the crack of rifle shots. Again the fugitive fled into the woods and evaded capture, only to sleep out in the wilderness. "Saturday morning, I walked toward Yocumtown and got something to eat from an old man who lives in the woods alone," Troup told his captors. "I slept along the edge of the pines for most of the day." On Sunday, Troup visited his brother-in-law, Clem Toomey, who convinced him to surrender. For the entire duration of the manhunt, Troup stayed in the same general area as the crime scene.

While in custody, Troup confessed to firing the fatal shot but declared that he didn't know that his victim was a police officer. He was home the night of the murder, playing cards with his sisters, Virginia and Hazel, his brother Walter and a friend named Norman "Pat" Wire. When someone knocked on the front door, Troup asked Virginia whether the back door was locked. He left the room to check, taking a shotgun with him. His story continues as follows:

> *The back door was closed, but not locked. I opened this door about one foot. There was no light outside. No moonlight. The only thing I saw was the gun. I could see no person's hands. I saw only the barrel of the revolver. I said "Don't shoot." Someone outside said "I might as well shoot you full of holes." No other words were exchanged.*

Rather than be shot, Troup fired off one quick blast with the shotgun and fled out of the house. He thought that the whole incident from start to finish took about five minutes. Troup maintained his story at trial the following August, adding that he thought the intruders might have been men from Virginia out to cause trouble. His father, Samuel, testified that some Virginians had come to the farm in the spring of 1928 and started a fight. Samuel did not elaborate on why but testified that he told his son what happened.

Prosecutor Amos Herrmann pressed for first-degree murder, arguing that Troup had made threats to shoot the first police officer who tried to arrest him on the theft charges. This proves premeditation, justifying a guilty verdict on the most serious charge. Wire testified that he and Troup went on a job-hunting trip to Virginia the week before the murder, during which Troup made the threat. Troup's card-playing relatives testified at the coroner's inquest that this same threat was made the night of the murder after the suspect had finished eating dinner. At trial, these witnesses changed their stories and denied ever hearing Troup make threats against police officers. "I was scared," sister Virginia said on the stand. "They had me scared and I didn't know what to say. The state police said if we didn't say the same as Pat, we'd all be locked up."

C.M. Baker, a justice of the peace in Emigsville, testified that in December 1928 he had prepared the original arrest warrant on the cattle thieves that did not include Jacob Troup's name. His name was added weeks later in January 1929, at a time when the victim, farmer Albert Toomey, was not present to authorize its insertion. Further, witnesses testified that Toomey, a relative of the cattle thieves, had decided to settle the matter out of court without the need to arrest the boys, who had agreed to pay fifty dollars in restitution for the calves they stole.

Defense attorney James Glessner argued that Sowers and the other officers had no legal information against his client and thus no basis for an arrest warrant. Thinking that the intruders were the men from Virginia who had made threats against his father, Jacob Troup acted in self-defense to protect himself, his home and his family. The arresting officers were treated the same as any other bandits or highwaymen, Glessner said.

The jury deliberated for only two hours before finding Troup guilty of first-degree murder on August 28, 1929. Glessner appealed the case, but the high court refused to grant Troup a new trial. He was sentenced to life but was released in 1940 after serving just over eleven years at Eastern State Penitentiary. Friends circulated a petition asking for his early release that was signed by many prominent Newberry Township residents.

Troup was jailed briefly in 1949 while the state investigated an alleged parole violation stemming from a quarrel between his sister and brother-in-law. The investigation found no evidence of bad behavior on the part of Troup, who had only intervened to spare his sister from being harmed.

"HERE IS A WARNING": THE DIETRICH FAMILY TRAGEDY

A bloody handprint on the wall was grim testimony that at least one child had put up a struggle. Crime scene investigators also noticed how a splotch of blood under an unoccupied bed indicated that ten-year-old Paul Dietrich suffered an axe blow to the head before hiding from his crazed father. But the death struggle was brief and in vain as the streaks of red were plainly leading from the bed to the boy's corpse lying next to the bedroom door. Harry Dietrich had been very thorough in his handiwork.

In all his experience as county coroner, Dr. L.U. Zech never came upon a more terrible example of violent death. He compared what he saw in that second-floor bedroom to the bloodletting of World War I. "The battlefields of France would hardly have produced a more ghastly spectacle than this human slaughterhouse," he said. The discovery broke records for Zech, who had to issue six death certificates in a single day—all for one family.

Jacob Eppley, a merchant in Spry, had an agreement with Harry Dietrich, a forty-two-year-old farmer who worked eighty acres just southwest of the village. Local residents remembered the killer as a thrifty, honest man who feared God and respected others. He was described by many as a good husband and a kind father. No wonder Eppley agreed to give the family man some groceries in exchange for ten bushels of potatoes. The store owner needed to replenish his stock. The deal was made just days before the September 21, 1930 mass murder.

That Tuesday, at about 3:00 p.m., Eppley began to wonder whether Dietrich had forgotten to deliver the potatoes. About an hour later, the merchant started out for the farm, figuring that he would bring back just enough spuds to fill the immediate need. Approaching the farm, Eppley heard a lot of noise coming from the hungry and restless livestock. He described what happened next: "I first went to the kitchen door and knocked. No one answered. I thought this strange, as usually some of the youngsters were found. Then I went to the barn, for the stock was carrying on. At the barn, I called for Dietrich."

Eppley then went to where the animals were kept, but the farmer was not there. Eppley went up on the barn floor, where he discovered Dietrich's body hanging from a beam. It appeared that the farmer had stepped off a ladder after placing a noose around his neck. Eppley drove to a nearby inn, where he phoned Zech, and together they returned to the farm to cut down the body that had been hanging there for more than a day. The neck was broken, and there were spots of blood on the farmer's shirt and overalls. But the blood was not Harry Dietrich's. In a pocket, investigators found a weird sketch resembling a noose drawn in a childish hand. This was the moment when the men first realized that something terrible had happened beyond a suicide.

Alarmed, they ran to the back porch and knocked on the kitchen door. No answer. They tried the door, found it unlocked and entered the farmhouse. There they saw in plain view an unsigned note scrawled in pencil and sitting atop an upturned candy box on the kitchen table. The message confirmed the worst: "Financial worry. Bury at Stone Pile cemetery…We decided to die together. I could not leave them alone."

Zech and Eppley conducted a search of every room downstairs and found nothing unusual. But when they searched the second floor, they found a door opened halfway and the almost unclothed body of Paul Dietrich, his head resting in a pool of blood that had soaked into the bare floorboards. What they discovered next left both men speechless. A reporter with the *Gazette and Daily* described it as follows: "With a brush dipped in blood, Death painted a scene of indescribable horror in the large bedroom on the second floor of the Dietrich home. There, besmeared with blood, the semi-nude bodies of the mother and her brood were found, rigid in varying positions as death came upon them."

Three beds stood along the western wall, all covered in blood. Two beds held the bodies of three children stretched across the covers in a manner that suggested they had offered no resistance. The children were eleven-year-old Mabel, eight-year-old Anna and five-year-old Johnnie. On the floor just inside the door were the bodies of Melvina Dietrich, age thirty-three, and her eldest son, Paul.

The newspaper reported how bloodstains were everywhere—on the walls, the furniture and the carpet. The mother was lying on her back in a pool of still moist blood that left the pattern on the rug beneath her unrecognizable. The men found the murder weapon lying nearby—its twenty-inch handle was covered with dried blood, while the butt end of the axe had evidence of human hair, blood and gray matter. There were obvious signs that Paul had probably crawled under the bed to escape his father but was dragged to his own untimely death.

The evidence suggested that Harry Dietrich had crept into the room after his family had gone to sleep. He then used the axe to administer one or more blows to the head, which had the effect of either stunning or killing each victim outright. To make doubly sure, and perhaps to prevent each victim from regaining consciousness, the farmer tied binder twine tightly around each throat using an iron pin from a bed frame to knot the death cord. The pin was found lying on the floor near Paul.

A closer examination confirmed that the mother and four children had each suffered a fractured skull that caused a concussion and cerebral hemorrhage. It appeared as though Melvina Dietrich and a daughter were hacked more than the others because large pieces of their skulls were displaced by the axe blows. His grim work done, Harry Dietrich went to the barn to hang himself.

As for motive, relatives knew that the farmer had been discouraged over the failure of most of his crop due to a prolonged summer drought. News of the tragedy devastated Dietrich's mother, who suffered under the enormity of the loss. "I knew something was wrong," she told a reporter between sobs. "Harry didn't act like himself when he was over to our place on Sunday afternoon. He wouldn't even come in the house to eat." Aaron Dietrich, his father, just wandered around in a daze.

Investigators combing through the house found an invoice from a Red Lion bank notifying the family that a $3,800 mortgage payment was due on September 27. Neighbors were convinced that his inability to pay this bill drove Harry Dietrich into such madness that he decided to destroy his family. The religious sayings and paintings on the walls indicated that the Dietrich family was Christian. It was reported how the children regularly attended Sunday school. On the bedroom wall was a painting of Jesus in prayer with the words, "Christ is the head of this home," in silver lettering. But it was the Dietrich family Bible that held the most important revelation.

In its pages, investigators found a neatly folded legal document entitled "Conditions of Sale of Personal Property," with blank spaces for the entry of names. It was later learned that Dietrich had visited a local realtor on Saturday, September 20—the day before he massacred his family. As he left the office, Dietrich gave instructions that a "for sale" sign be posted in the lane leading up to the farm. This Bible also yielded the following poem written and signed by Mabel Dietrich, the eldest daughter:

Some little folks are apt to say when asked their task to touch,
I'll put it off at least today, it cannot matter much.
Time is always on the wing, you cannot stop its flight;
Then do at once your little task, you'll happier be at night.

A closer inspection showed that the farm was in good condition. The barn was well stocked. There were plenty of canned goods in storage.

The smokehouse had an abundance of meat. Neighbors came to feed the hungry animals, which included four horses, two mules, four cows and lots of chickens. There were even two dogs, including a friendly shepherd who wagged his tail at the sight of visitors.

Word spread rapidly of the tragedy, drawing the morbidly curious from all over the county to the farm. State troopers were dispatched for traffic control, while newspaper reporters phoned the farmhouse hungry for the details. As night approached, investigators were left milling in the dark in a home that had no electricity. Efforts to light the oil lamps proved futile because Dietrich had used up all the fuel during his murder spree.

In the days that followed, relatives maintained a strict vigil over the farm, only allowing those having business with the estate onto the property. The newspaper reported how relatives burned the bloodstained bed clothing and furniture. Relatives also installed new flooring and wallpaper to cover up any sign of the murders.

The *York Dispatch* reported how about five thousand people attended the October 11, 1930 sale of the Dietrich farm. The event took on a country fair atmosphere, with people lining up to catch glimpses of the second-floor bedroom. Bidding started at noon and continued until about 7:30 p.m. Elmer Markey bought the farm for $4,500; the personal property sold for $1,959. "A number of axes were sold…but it was said none of them was the one used by Dietrich to crush out the life of his family," the *Dispatch* reported. Proceeds from the sale were more than enough to liquidate the bank debt.

Press reports vary, but as many as four thousand people may have viewed the bodies prior to burial in the Bethlehem Evangelical Cemetery near Springvale in Windsor Township. This was the cemetery Harry Dietrich was referring to in his note found on the kitchen table. The caskets were arranged by age and lowered into a single grave. The service was held on September 25, 1930, with the sermon being delivered by Reverend M.B. Heiland, a pastor of the Red Lion United Brethren circuit. Heiland had not only officiated over the wedding of Melvina Runkle and Harry Dietrich, but he also baptized the father and each of the children. Heiland also served as a clerk during the subsequent property sale.

In his sermon, "The Uncertainty of Life," Heiland avoided any direct reference to the crime, preferring instead to assuage the grief of the family by talking of the living instead of the dead. He drew heavily from Mark 13:33: "Take ye heed, watch and pray, for ye know not when the time is." The following are excerpts from his message:

This photograph shows the headstone for the Dietrich family, with the six individual grave markers of the family members in the foreground. *Photo by Joseph Cress.*

> *For man, death chooses all seasons. The cradle is his. Childhood and youth are his; the laughing eye is quenched, the gleeful shout is hushed. The prime of manhood and womanhood is his; he blights the freshness of hope and promises and clothes in the garments of the grave those bound most closely by the ties of life. He often sends no summons before him, but floats unseen on the breeze and has aimed his shaft before his approach is perceived…*
>
> *Here is a warning: "With all of man's wisdom, and understanding and knowledge, there is one thing his mind cannot fathom. He does not know when the end shall be"…*
>
> *No matter how our earthly life shall come to a close; no matter when our life shall end, let us watch and pray, let us take heed.*

PART VI
UNSOLVED

There will always be mysteries, cases without closure. These are stories of corpses crying out for justice even as the evidence trail grows colder with each passing year. Memory fails. Witnesses die off. Killers succeed in taking their dirty secrets to the grave. And the victims…well, they may never truly rest in peace. We begin with a young mother found bludgeoned to death in a lonely hollow. We then travel to the city for the story of an eccentric whose quirky personality traits sealed his fate. We end the book as it began, with the death of innocence and the discovery of a young woman's body on the railroad tracks.

"Murder Hole": The Pigeon Hills Slaying

The first assault was made with a small club, or so the theory went. Christiana Harman had just walked by the spring along the side of the gloomy hollow when a killer struck her down. Here the road between Jacobs Mills and High Rock in Heidelberg Township was steep and rocky—barely wide enough for a single wagon. The hollow was flanked on both sides by high hills covered with rocks, thick woods and dense undergrowth. No wonder it went by the name "Murder Hole."

Investigators piecing together the clues at the scene theorized that the murderer approached Harman from her right side, hitting the top of her head with a downward blow. The impact knocked her down and caused the butt end of the club to break off and fly in a straight line. Dazed, the unwed mother of two small children stood up. She either screamed or tried to, but her cries for help were cut off when her killer clubbed her across the face, breaking her jaw and slashing her chin.

Frustrated, the murderer tossed the light club aside and looked around for something heavier. It was after 10:00 p.m. on December 7, 1878, and the moon was bright enough to help in the search. Meanwhile, Harman began to stagger off toward her home, which was about four hundred yards away. Blinded by the blood flow, the thirty-two-year-old woman was probably going on gut instinct or force of habit. She had lived in that part of the Pigeon Hills all her life.

The theory goes that the mystery killer found a large piece of heavy oak and rushed after the victim. Investigators believed that Harman looked back and that the fatal blow landed directly on her forehead, knocking her lifeless to the ground. One would think that would be enough, but the killer kept right on clubbing the victim. The force of his blows shattered almost every bone in her skull, left her brain exposed and hammered a two-inch impression into the soil beneath her head. But it didn't end there. The murderer fired a single bullet through her right eye, singeing her eyebrow and leaving gunpowder residue in the wound. The flattened hunk of lead was recovered from a stone found under Harman at the crime scene.

Traveler Edmund Stouffer found her body at about 8:00 a.m. on Sunday, sprawled out across the road about three-fourths of a mile northwest of Moulstown. He pressed on to the village to report his discovery. Several men hurried to the scene, including Wiley Gemmil, who identified the victim by her bloody shawl. He could not recognize her face. Harman was lying on her back in mud and slush, her head resting on a stone in the middle of the road. Her arms were drawn up across her chest, and the white mitten on her left hand was soaked with blood.

There was no evidence of robbery or rape. The bundles of merchandise that Harman had purchased in Hanover that Saturday were scattered about the crime scene, including a new pair of shoes. Her clothing was undisturbed, and her only injury was the head trauma. There were fragments of a chestnut club lying near her hat, which was located about nine yards from her body. The butt end of this weapon was found about five yards up the hill. The evidence suggested that this club was freshly cut from a tree stump located farther up the road.

Investigators also found a heavy oak club about thirty to forty feet off the road opposite to where the hat was located. It was bloody, with hair sticking on it. Frederick Harman, father of Christiana, recalled dropping this piece of wood from his wagon several days before the murder. The shoe prints of both the killer and the victim were plainly visible. Here the frozen ground was softened by the flowing spring water. There was a blood trail leading from the hat to the body.

News of the murder spread rapidly, and soon hundreds of people had visited the crime scene—many coming in from far away. Some swore vengeance against the killer, and there were reports that search parties bent on vigilante justice were being formed to hunt down the prime suspect, Ephraim Snyder, who was later charged with the murder. He had frequently visited the victim in the five years leading up to her death.

Frederick Harman would testify how Snyder would show up at the family home at intervals two to four weeks apart, arriving at different times of the day. Often his daughter and Snyder went for walks along the road for half a day at a time. When they returned, she would go back into the house, while Snyder would continue down the road. Sometimes he would stay and visit until 4:00 a.m. Mr. Harman recalled how Snyder was away in Kansas for much of 1877. When he returned to Pennsylvania, the suspect went to visit Christiana. At that time, her father asked Snyder how he liked Kansas. Snyder responded that he would be happy if he had Annie to keep house for him. The father said that the last time the suspect had visited Christiana was in early November 1878.

The day she died, Christiana left home at about 8:00 a.m. to walk to Hanover, where she purchased the shoes and calico fabric. She left town about 5:00 p.m. and about ninety minutes later arrived at the home of Reuben Snyder, where neighbors had gathered for a singing—a common social activity of the time. Witnesses set her departure at about 9:00 p.m. It was the last time Christiana Harman was seen alive by anyone who would admit it.

When arrested, Snyder denied any involvement in her death and told investigators that he had not arranged a meeting with her the night she was killed. He testified that he had left his home that evening to attend a singing at a nearby school but only stayed about half an hour before leaving because the attendance was poor. He then started to walk toward a religious meeting at a nearby church but turned back partway there because he heard hallooing and thought that the meeting was over. Snyder said that he saw no one on his way home and claimed that he had last seen the victim during the harvest.

Indeed, the evidence against Snyder was purely circumstantial. The bullet recovered from the crime scene had as much lead as the bullets in a revolver that the accused kept in his room. A close examination of his clothes found only a small spot of blood on a pocket, which Snyder said was from a sore finger. His boots were soiled with mud similar to what was found at the scene.

The prevailing theory as to motive was that Snyder was having sex with the victim out of wedlock and that she was using a pregnancy to force their marriage when he planned to marry another woman. The prosecution pushed the notion that Christiana had threatened to reveal his indiscretions, thus jeopardizing his wedding plans set for the week after Christmas.

Two witnesses testified in support of this theory: Margaret Harman, the victim's mother, and Rebecca Snyder, the suspect's sister-in-law and a first cousin to Christiana. The mother said that she saw her daughter and Ephraim talk at a fence near the Harman family home about a week before the murder. She did not overhear the conversation but assumed that the topic was marriage. The cousin testified that Christiana had told her she was in a "situation" and that if Ephraim didn't marry her she would "know what to do." This theory was dismissed after the autopsy revealed that the victim was not pregnant at the time of her death. In his instructions to the jury, Judge Pere Wickes explained the importance of motive in fixing guilt: "Men in civilized communities do not cruelly take human life without some powerful motive…Underlying all crime of his character was some human passion, anger, hatred, revenge, jealousy or some kindred passion almost invariable breed in the heart where murder is conceived."

Judge Pere Wickes. *From the collection of the York County Heritage Trust, York, Pennsylvania.*

The judge also reminded jurors about the defendant's alibi. Testimony set the time of the murder as being after 10:00 p.m., when witnesses placed Ephraim Snyder in bed about a quarter of a mile from the crime scene. A neighbor testified to hearing dogs barking and a single gunshot at about 10:30 p.m. Margaret Harman said that she heard a similar disturbance at about 10:00 p.m. when her son, Solomon, returned from his nighttime excursions. "The dogs made an awful noise and went on dreadfully," she would testify in court.

The night of the murder, Ephraim Snyder was staying with his boss, Nathaniel Moul. Elizabeth Moul, the wife, testified that the suspect left the home early that evening and returned between 9:30 and 10:00 p.m. She told jurors that he came into the kitchen, removed his coat and jacket and pulled off his boots. The suspect then played briefly with one of her sons before going into a different room, where he drank cider before heading off to bed.

An observant juror noticed that the bullets found in the suspect's cartridge box were of a different design than the bullet found at the crime scene. All of this was enough to convince the jury that too much reasonable doubt existed to find Ephraim Snyder guilty of the crime.

"Wrapped in Horror": A Crime Scene Sketch

It was only a nightmare. It just had to be, but false hope can give way to lingering regret. Anna Herman heard her uncle cry out for help, but she stayed in bed, too terrified to move. Instead, she drew small comfort from the light shining through the transom above his door. She figured that David Heckert was just trying to settle himself after a rude awakening. Yet Herman could not completely shake the nagging suspicion that something out of the ordinary was happening in the bedroom down the hall. So she watched the light for about an hour until it disappeared. Then she heard the sound of a window being raised and lowered in her uncle's room. Unbeknownst to her, a murderer had left the building, along with the best opportunity to solve a mystery.

It was about 11:30 p.m. on Friday, February 14, 1908. Herman and Salome Heckert were ready to retire for the night when they saw the light in their uncle's room go dark. They figured that he must have gone to bed. Then, just after midnight, the nieces heard the cries, "Murder! Murder! Help! Help!" coming from down the hallway. Salome thought that if she could only get out of her bed, she could open her room window and summon help. Their home at 48 East Market Street was about 120 feet from police headquarters and located along a busy thoroughfare in downtown York city. But Salome was paralyzed with fear. Fifteen minutes after the cries pierced the night, the women saw the bedroom light shine through the transom, leading them to believe in false hope. Salome went back to sleep, but Herman stayed awake the whole night.

The *York Gazette* reported how the murder of David Heckert left the community "wrapped in horror at the terrible deed" and in the dark as to the perpetrator. The eighty-two-year-old victim was generally well liked and possessed a great sense of humor. A retired plumber and tinsmith, he was ambitious and owned property in the city. As a hobby, he delighted in drawing caricatures of friends along with sketches showing the funny side of everyday life from his memories of growing up in York during the nineteenth century. Two of his drawings are included in this book.

However, there were characteristics in his personality that set him up to be a victim and would work against investigators trying to solve his murder. David Heckert mistrusted banks, and it was common knowledge that he kept money in his room. The quirky eccentric paid all of his bills with cash stored in a cigar box located in the closet. After his death, family members

This image shows David Heckert with snowmen that he sculpted following a snowfall. *From the collection of the York County Heritage Trust, York, Pennsylvania.*

noticed how the closet door was left open. This was something that the victim would never have allowed even for spring and fall cleanup. The family suspected that the murder was the result of a robbery gone bad. Evidence at the scene suggested that David Heckert woke up and discovered the intruder, who, in turn, went up to the bed and struck the old man on the head with a blunt instrument.

The secretive nature of the victim made it impossible for police to estimate how much money was stolen. This did not stop wild speculation on the street that the hidden treasure trove had contained as much as $50,000. Investigators searching the room found no money in the cigar box but did find more than $3,000 in gold coins and currency wrapped in newspapers beneath a pile of rubbish in the victim's closest. This money was later distributed to relatives as part of the estate.

Another personality quirk delayed the start of the investigation. It was believed that the murder took place between midnight and 1:00 a.m. on February 15, 1908, but the body was not discovered for another nine hours. This was because the victim was in the habit of staying in his room until about 10:00 or 11:00 a.m. and became angry if anyone disturbed him before that time. The women knew that but also remembered his cries for help, so when their uncle didn't appear by 8:00 a.m., they began to panic.

Even then, they didn't raise the alarm but instead waited until Edward Heckert arrived to open his shop at the rear of the house. Well aware of his uncle's quirkiness, the nephew dismissed their concern and instead went out on an errand to repair a leak. When Edward returned at about 10:00 a.m., he saw that the women were still concerned, but he was unable to enter his uncle's room. The victim was also in the habit of locking all of his doors and windows at bedtime.

David Small ran a candy store in the same building, so the family recruited him to climb a ladder and look through the transom into the room. "My God, there is blood on the bed," Small said. He was sure that the old man was dead. The crime was reported to police, who entered the room and found David Heckert lying on his back surrounded by blood-soaked pillows and blankets. Only his head and lower right leg were exposed.

Investigators developed a theory based on the evidence. They believed that the robber had struck Heckert a couple of times on the head when the victim first cried out. After searching the room, the robber returned to the bed, grabbed the unconscious man by the hair and struck him four to five more times to make sure that he was dead. The body had eight cuts on top of the forehead inflicted by a blunt instrument. The autopsy revealed

Interior of David Heckert's room—scene of his murder. *From the collection of the York County Heritage Trust, York, Pennsylvania.*

that Heckert did not die from the head trauma but rather bled out slowly for hours.

There was speculation the murderer was not a professional criminal but rather an amateur caught in the act and possibly recognized by Heckert. Police believed that the intruder had no intention of killing the victim but rather committed the crime out of nervous energy and fear of prosecution. They based this conclusion on the wound pattern. Eight blows were delivered, yet the skull was not crushed, indicating that the weapon used was lightweight and may have been something handy like a screwdriver. A professional would have bound and gagged Heckert or would have used a blackjack or similar weapon to stun or kill the old man without leaving a visible trace.

Investigators also believed that the killer was someone familiar with the family who knew that Herman and Salome Heckert would be too scared to intervene. They suspected that this person also knew that Jacob Heckert was completely deaf and would have slept through any commotion coming from his brother's adjoining room. The problem was that too many people in the city knew the victim and his family. So finding the weapon was the key to solving the murder.

The killer left few clues behind. "The robber displayed tidiness worthy of a housekeeper," the *Gazette* reported. There was evidence that the intruder went through dresser drawers but that everything had been replaced neatly. The cigar box had checks and receipts but no money. At first, investigators believed that the blood on the blankets was from the killer wiping off the murder weapon, but they later found fingerprints on the bedding and on a wall. While some believed that usable prints could have been recovered, others thought the one blanket was handled by so many people that it was nearly worthless as a reliable source of evidence.

In the closet, police found a bloodstained towel hidden behind a row of bottles and a basin of water. It appeared that someone had tried to wash blood from their hands before wiping the stains off on the towel. The room yielded one other clue. One of the south-side windows was unlatched and showed evidence of tampering. A ladder behind the house showed marks of having been moved recently. One theory was that the robber used the ladder to access the balcony that surrounded the room. Police also questioned a suspect who was caught with a skeleton key, but there was no specific mention of that person being arrested.

Investigators found a brick in the backyard with traces of hair and blood, indicating that someone may have wiped a hand across it. A property search turned up no sign of the murder weapon, leading investigators to believe that the killer may have dropped it down a backyard well. Police used grappling hooks to dredge the bottom of the fifty-foot well, without success. The newspaper speculated that the weapon may never be found.

This case drew so much attention that city police assigned a detail to control the crowd that had gathered outside the victim's home for the funeral. The service was private, with only the immediate family invited. In his eulogy, Reverend T.T. Everett had this to say: "The guilty may escape human detection, but not the all-seeing eye of their Maker. In the last analysis, He cannot be baffled...Every unpunished murderer takes away something from the security of every man's life."

Police received calls from all over the city from people claiming that they saw suspicious men near the Heckert home the night of the murder. William Henze of York was passing by the residence about midnight when he saw two men standing on the front steps. They turned their backs as he approached and spoke in whispers. After walking by, Henze looked back and saw the men walk down the steps and toward the Square. He described one

A drawing of a lawyer done by David Heckert. *From the collection of the York County Heritage Trust, York, Pennsylvania.*

as being stout and about fifty years old, while the other seemed younger and taller. Henze was unable to positively identify a suspect in a lineup who had a handkerchief in his possession with gray hairs resembling the victim's. In another sighting, Otto Baughman, a messenger boy for the Postal Telegraph Company, saw a man in the alley behind the Heckert place at about 11:00 p.m. on Friday night. Nothing definitive came out of either of these tips.

Suspects included John Heckert, who had purchased a revolver from a pawn shop the same morning his uncle's body was found. The nephew had no visible reaction when store clerk Alex Kagen said, "We have to be careful these days with things going on like the murder of old man Heckert." Kagen also noticed how the nephew paid with cash unrolled from a large quantity of bills.

On March 7, 1908, John Heckert fired a single shot from this same revolver down Mason Alley while he was chasing after an alleged thief. Edward Strine told police how Heckert was passed out drunk on a bench in front of the Motter House hotel with a bundle containing shoes. Strine thought that it would be a good joke to steal the bundle and then hide it. His valuables gone, Heckert recovered quickly and gave chase, firing a bullet that missed Strine. Only a minute later, a wagon containing a family passed down the alley in a direct line with its trajectory. Heckert was arrested.

Conflicting stories on the purchase of the gun fueled suspicion and led police to investigate John Heckert. In one story, the nephew said that he bought the gun from a manufacturer in Connecticut, but he declined to give names. The suspect told relatives that he acquired the gun in 1906 from a cavalry soldier camped out on the fairgrounds. Though his story was convoluted, investigators could not shatter his alibi.

John Heckert told police that he was home from 5:00 p.m. the night of the murder until later the next morning. His parents and two sisters corroborated this statement. John Baughman, proprietor of the Baughman House Inn, told police that John Heckert was in the barroom at about midnight the morning the murder was committed. Baughman was so confident in his recollection that he even mentioned the brand of beer John Heckert bought.

"This Darkest of Mysteries": The Murder of Gertrude Rudy

It was meant to look like an accident. Whoever brutally murdered Gertrude Rudy wanted her body to be mangled under the steel wheels of a passing train, but fate intervened and set York city police on the path of an unsolved mystery. Detectives were diligent. They chased down multiple leads, but no charges were ever filed. Investigators even questioned the prime suspect in a far more notorious killing on his alleged connections to the girl. Nothing ever came of it. As with other murders, the shock faded away, the trail went cold and survivors were left to wonder why their loved one was dead.

At about 9:00 p.m. on November 11, 1927, W. Dupes was walking along the tracks of the Maryland and Pennsylvania Railroad on his way to the Spring Garden brickyard, where he spent his nights. About one thousand feet from his destination, he came upon the mutilated body of a teenage girl laid across the rails. He pressed on to notify workers at the brickyard. Within minutes, the crime scene was swarming with police, derelicts and curious spectators. Witnesses were careful to first remove the body from the tracks to save it from a train.

Evidence at the scene convinced police that the murder had taken place elsewhere and that the body had been dragged to the tracks to conceal the crime. The most telling evidence of a body dump was in her badly mangled and broken jaw that had been hacked by a cleaver or similar instrument. Such an injury would have bled profusely, yet there was little blood at the scene.

The autopsy revealed that the girl had suffered an extensive laceration of her chin and lower jaw and that the roof of her mouth had been fractured. A bullet had entered her left breast between the fifth and sixth ribs before passing through her left lung and tearing away that side of her heart. It appeared as though a blunt instrument may have caused a wound about an inch wide on the top-left part of her head. The girl was six to eight weeks pregnant.

Residents of nearby Spring Garden Township had heard two to three gunshots at about 7:30 p.m. that evening. Investigators searching the body found the means to identify the victim in an inside coat pocket. It was a small bottle wrapped in gift paper with the inscription, "To Neal Stough from Gertrude Rudy." The newspaper did not specify what was in the bottle. Police questioned the fifteen-year-old boy, but there were no reports of any details. In a pocket of her dress, police found thirty cents wrapped in a handkerchief. Her glasses were on her face.

Probing deeper, investigators learned that Rudy had visited a local doctor just days before her murder to seek an abortion. The doctor discouraged her from having the procedure. She was accompanied by a male companion who had been charged with rape some time ago "by those interested in Miss Rudy," reported the *Gazette and Daily*. Police questioned her companion and cleared him of murder when it was proven that he was elsewhere at the time of the crime.

Police diagrammed the girl's movements the night of her murder. She left home on East King Street at about 7:00 p.m. and walked west on Princess Street to the home of Elwood Einsig, with whom she had a conversation. She then crossed the street to travel east on Princess before crossing back over again. She was last seen alive on the south side of the 900 block of East Princess Street.

As per the custom of the day, the viewing and funeral services were held in the dead girl's home. A crowd of just over five thousand toured the overcrowded residence. Police could not have known that one of these visitors was a man named John Blymyer, a powwow doctor arrested a year later in the murder of Nelson Rehmeyer. The infamous Hex Murder was featured earlier in this book.

Almost five months later, on April 5, 1928, the *Gazette and Daily* ran an article explaining how there were no new developments in the Rudy murder:

"Investigating officers seem to find insurmountable objects to all clues which they thought might…solve this darkest of mysteries." District Attorney Amos Herrmann assigned eight detectives from York city and county to work the case until it was solved. The county commissioners posted a reward of $300—the modern equivalent of $3,782—for information leading to an arrest.

Despite the bleak progress, relatives were confident that police were doing everything they could to bring the killer to justice. Family members were convinced that a Chevrolet sedan seen near the Rudy home the night of the murder and early the next morning was driven by someone with knowledge of the crime. The car had stopped several times near the house and had repeatedly passed by on the street. Police officers living in the area made several attempts to get a look at the driver, but each time he drove away just before anyone could approach him in the darkness. The whole time, the police and family were given false leads by an unnamed source who boasted that he would only give correct information if the county commissioners increased the reward to $500.

The same newspaper on April 12 reported how an alleged witness to the Rudy murder had been arrested recently on an unrelated charge of lewdness. Paul "Dummy" Long, a mute, was put in jail while police investigated a claim by a woman that he had made inappropriate advances toward two teenage girls picking dandelions close to where Rudy's body was found. The morning after the murder, Long told police in pantomime that he had seen Rudy walking behind a man along the railroad tracks the night before.

Long followed them and watched as the man turned around and fired a single shotgun shell into her chest before hitting her on the head with the firearm. Long would later change his story, saying that it was too dark to see the murder. His credibility was further damaged by another witness, who told police that the mute had "the imaginative mind of a child" that caused him to embellish stories as a ploy to get attention.

Seven months later, John Blymyer was arrested on charges that he had murdered Nelson Rehmeyer. As police delved deeper into the Hex Murder, they also questioned Blymyer on the Rudy case. While he admitted to knowing the girl, Blymyer denied any knowledge of her murder, but it was reported that he was "plainly uncomfortable" under the direct examination of York city detective W.H. Myers, chief investigator in the Rudy homicide. "Shortly after the interview began, streams of perspiration began pouring down his face," a reporter described Blymyer.

The Hex Murder investigation generated fresh leads on the Rudy homicide, giving that cold case renewed vigor even as police uncovered connections between the girl, Blymyer and the mystery sedan. But there was never enough evidence to charge Blymyer with her murder. That didn't prevent the *York Dispatch* from building up hype on the connections as illustrated by this excerpt from a December 4, 1928 story: "The hand of guilt…appears to be reaching through the bars of the York County jail to tighten the fingers of evidence upon John Blymyer…Each hour is revealing new facts which police believe may finally link Blymyer with the Rudy girl's death."

For one thing, Blymyer admitted that he once worked as a cigar maker in the same Beaver Street factory where Rudy was an employee. The suspect claimed that he had been working at a local hosiery factory the night of her murder. His work record at the plant showed that he was not an employee there in the five weeks before the Rudy murder. Blymyer also told police that at the time of her murder he lived at two different addresses near the East King Street home of Gertrude Rudy. His address on East Mason Alley was near where one of her closest friends lived and was one of the homes the victim had visited the night she was killed. His other address was in the 600 block of East Princess Street.

Blymyer told police that he attended Rudy's funeral out of curiosity, accompanied by his sister Minnie Olewiler, but she told investigators that she had not been with her brother but rather had learned of his visit to the funeral through relatives. The most damaging links between Blymyer and Rudy came out of interviews the police had with John Goodling and his fifteen-year-old son, William. The father said that at the time of the Rudy murder they were living on the 600 block of East Princess Street, where they rented a room to Blymyer. Several times, phone calls came into the home asking for John Albright—an alias Blymyer used as a powwow doctor. When John Goodling told the caller that there was no one living there by that name, the caller would almost always say, "I mean the powwow doctor." Then Goodling would call Blymyer to the phone.

There were times during the course of these conversations that John Goodling heard Blymyer mention the name "Gertrude," though he never heard a last name spoken. John Goodling added that most of the patients Blymyer saw as a powwow doctor were women. His son William said that he once saw Gertrude Rudy in Blymyer's room. He knew her because they attended the same school. Investigators had a theory that after the doctor had refused to give Rudy an abortion, she turned to witchcraft as her only remaining remedy for her pregnancy. What's more, John Goodling told police that Blymyer was not in his room the night of the girl's murder. At about 1:00 a.m. on November 12, 1927, John Goodling answered a phone call from a person wanting the services of the powwow doctors, but when Goodling went to summon Blymyer, the suspect was not in his room. He only appeared again at 3:00 p.m. that afternoon.

During their interview with Blymyer, police asked him whether he owned an automobile. He told investigators that he never owned or driven a car—nor could he drive even. However, William Goodling told police that he had seen Blymyer operate a rental car described as a Ford sedan the night the Rudy girl was killed. This statement was substantiated by a police visit to the Deardorff Auto Livery, where two employees remembered that Blymyer had rented cars from the company. However, police could not verify this because the records for November 1927 had been destroyed, and the Ford sedan that Blymyer may have rented had since been disposed of.

BIBLIOGRAPHY

Bitter Divides

"One Common Ruin": The Negro Conspiracy of 1803

Carter W.C., and A. J. Glossbrenner. *History of York County*. Baltimore, MD: Baltimore Regional Publishing Co., 1975.

York Recorder. "Another Dreadful Fire." March 16, 1803.

———. "Another Fire!!!" March 9, 1803.

———. "Conspiracy of the Negroes." March 29, 1825.

———. "Fire!" March 2, 1803.

———. "Fire!!" March 9, 1803.

———. "A Proclamation." March 23, 1803.

———. "Those Black Miscreants." May 25, 1803.

———. "To…Inhabitants of the Borough." March 30, 1803.

———. "Tranquility…Gradually Returning." March 23, 1803.

Bitter Divides Introduction and York Race Riot Sections

Argento, Mike. "Their Tearful Best." *York Daily Record*, October 21, 2002.

Argento, Mike, and Rick Lee. "A Surprise to the Last." *York Daily Record*, April 15, 2004.

Boeckel, Teresa. "Feast Remembers Two Victims." *York Daily Record*, February 4, 2002.

———. "He Rode Beside Schaad." *York Daily Record*, March 7, 2003.

Boeckel, Teresa, and Jim Lynch. "Delving into Delays." *York Daily Record*, March 1, 2003.

———. "Family Wants Questions About Police Answered." *York Daily Record*, October 10, 2002.

———. "Files Show FBI Kept Tabs on York During Race Riots." *York Daily Record.*

———. "Henry Schaad and Lilli Belle Allen Are Linked by Violent Chapter of York's History." *York Daily Record*, February 28, 2003.

———. "Officer's Kin Prepares for Trial." *York Daily Record*, March 1, 2003.

———. "Tales Differ on the Stand." *York Daily Record*, October 3, 2002.

———. "Talk of Barricade Opens Day One." *York Daily Record*, October 2, 2002.

Boeckel, Teresa, and Rick Lee. "Jury Hears Case." *York Daily Record*, March 6, 2003.

———. "Making the Case." *York Daily Record*, October 11, 2002.

———. "Witness Stuns Court." *York Daily Record*, March 7, 2003.

Boeckel, Teresa, Rick Lee and Jim Lynch. "Another Chapter Closes." *York Daily Record*, December 19, 2002.

———. "Best Evidence Lost." *York Daily Record*, October 16, 2002.

———. "Cop: I Moved Barricade." *York Daily Record*, October 8, 2002.

———. "Cops of '69 on Trial." *York Daily Record*, October 9, 2002.

———. "Defense Attacks Witnesses' Credibility." *York Daily Record*, March 8, 2003.

———. "Fear and Confusion Filled the Street." *York Daily Record*, October 16, 2002.

———. "Messersmith Blames Police, Others in Court." *York Daily Record*, December 19, 2002.

———. "Messersmith Recalls Two Nights." *York Daily Record*, October 5, 2002.

———. "On His Own Behalf." *York Daily Record*, March 12, 2003.

———. "The Prosecution Rests." *York Daily Record*, October 11, 2002.

———. "Schaad Finale Nears." *York Daily Record*, March 11, 2003.

———. "Two Witnesses Say Suspect Bragged." *York Daily Record*, October 10, 2002.

———. "White Power Rally Relived." *York Daily Record*, October 3, 2003.

———. "Witness's Memory Falters." *York Daily Record*, October 4, 2002.

———. "Witnesses Detail Murder." *York Daily Record*, October 9, 2003.

Boeckel, Teresa, Shawn Ledington, Rick Lee and Jim Lynch. "D.A., Defense Attorneys Sketch Out Battle Plans." *York Daily Record*, October 2, 2002.

Broman, Andrew. "Robertson Looks Forward." *York Daily Record*, October 21, 2002.

Evans, Elizabeth. "Allen Shooter Dies in Jail." *York Dispatch*, December 20, 2005.

———. "City Police Breathe Sigh of Relief." *York Dispatch*, March 14, 2003.

———. "Schaad Family Feels Relief and Redemption." *York Dispatch*, March 14, 2003.

Himmelright, Wendi, and Mark Scolforo. "Lawyers Differ on Race Issue." *York Dispatch*, March 6, 2003.

Hoover, Mike. "Allen's Family Sues York." *York Dispatch*, January 29, 2003.

———. "Brother: We All Shot at Car." *York Dispatch*, March 7, 2003.

———. "Council Backs Deal." *York Daily Record*, December 7, 2005.

———. "Messersmith Admits Role." *York Dispatch*, August 30, 2002.

———. "Prosecutors Say Witnesses…Will Be Tough to Sell." *York Dispatch*, March 2, 2003.

———. "Race Issue Could Affect Outcome." *York Dispatch*, March 5, 2003.

———. "Thieves, Scoundrels." *York Dispatch*, March 4, 2003.

Hoover, Mike, and Lauri Lebo. "Goodling: Trial May Bring Violence." *York Sunday News*, October 13, 2002.

———. "More Point Finger at Messersmith." *York Dispatch*, October 10, 2002.

Hoover, Mike, and Mark Scolforo. "After 33 Years, a Trial." *York Dispatch*, October 1, 2002.

———. "Officer: No One Was Shooting from 'Big Al.'" *York Dispatch*, March 7, 2003.

———. "Testimony on Officer at Center of Attention." *York Dispatch*, October 6, 2002.

———. "Two Convicted in Cop Killing." *York Dispatch*, March 14, 2003.

Klimanis, Daina. "Allen Family to Get $1.3M." *York Dispatch*, June 21, 2006.

Lebo, Lauri. "Clear Snapshot of Officer's Death Still Elusive." *York Dispatch*, March 2, 2003.

———. "Daughter: Sentences Too Lenient." *York Dispatch*, November 14, 2002.

———. "Defense: It Was Justified by the Times." *York Dispatch*, October 18, 2002.

———. "Roots of Fear, Hatred Buried Deep." *York Dispatch*, September 22, 2002.

Ledington, Shawn. "Acquittal Disappoints Many." *York Daily Record*, October 21, 2002.

Lee, Rick. "City, Family Settle." *York Daily Record*, December 7, 2005.
———. "Former Police Officer Takes the Stand." *York Daily Record*, March 6, 2003.
———. "Riot Death Appeals Rejected." *York Daily Record*, October 21, 2004.
Lee, Rick, and Jim Lynch. "Four Plea in 1969 Case." *York Daily Record*, August 15, 2002.
Rappold, R. Scott, and Charlie Young. "Still, It's the Prism of Race." *York Dispatch*, March 14, 2003.
Scolforo, Mark. "Allen Defendants' Fate Now Up to the Jury." *York Dispatch*, October 18, 2002.
———. "Assistant DA Takes on Critics in Letter." *York Dispatch*, November 15, 2002.
———. "Most May Spend Less than a Year in York County Jail." *York Dispatch*, November 14, 2002.
———. "Witnesses Describe Attacks in Penn-College Area." *York Dispatch*, March 6, 2003.
York Daily Record. "Death Claims Defendants." August 18, 2006.

Fistfights and Firewater

"Theater of Their Unblushing Defiance": The Goldsboro Prizefight

True Democrat. "An Outrage." January 22, 1867.
———. "Correction." January 29, 1867.
———. "Prize Fight at Goldsboro." January 22, 1867.
York County Star. "Belligerent." January 25, 1867.
York Gazette. "Prize Fight." January 15, 1867.
———. "Prize Fight." January 22, 1867.

"Fatal Lack of Continuity": The Pleasureville Brawl

York Daily. "Confessed to Several." November 20, 1907.
———. "Coroner's Jury Renders Verdict." November 22, 1907.
———. "Murder Charge Against Youths." November 19, 1907.
York Dispatch. "Double Murder Two Brothers." November 18, 1907.
———. "Snyder Is Guilty." November 19, 1907.
———. "Strong Evidence Needed at Hearing." November 22, 1907.

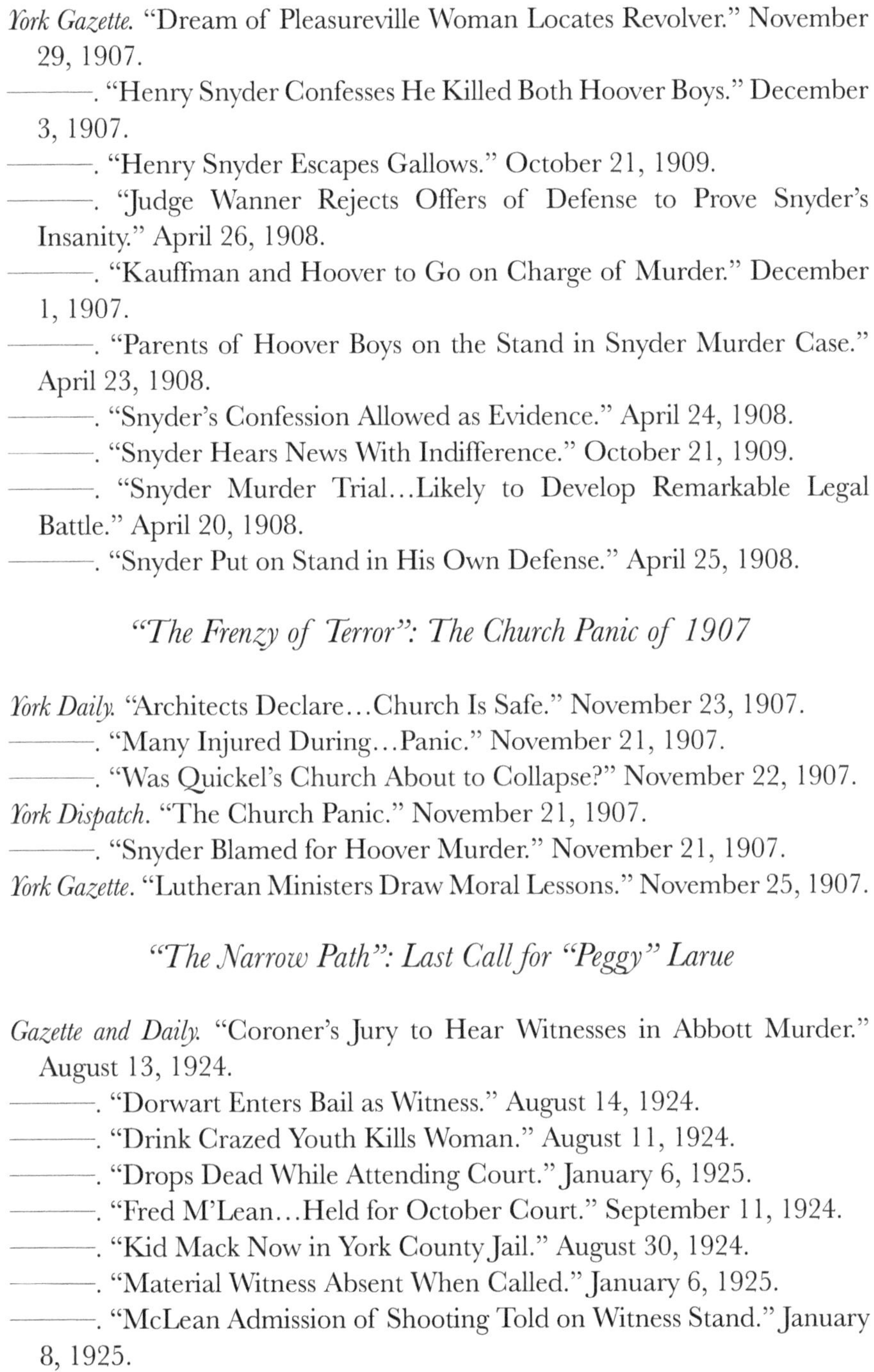

York Gazette. "Dream of Pleasureville Woman Locates Revolver." November 29, 1907.

———. "Henry Snyder Confesses He Killed Both Hoover Boys." December 3, 1907.

———. "Henry Snyder Escapes Gallows." October 21, 1909.

———. "Judge Wanner Rejects Offers of Defense to Prove Snyder's Insanity." April 26, 1908.

———. "Kauffman and Hoover to Go on Charge of Murder." December 1, 1907.

———. "Parents of Hoover Boys on the Stand in Snyder Murder Case." April 23, 1908.

———. "Snyder's Confession Allowed as Evidence." April 24, 1908.

———. "Snyder Hears News With Indifference." October 21, 1909.

———. "Snyder Murder Trial…Likely to Develop Remarkable Legal Battle." April 20, 1908.

———. "Snyder Put on Stand in His Own Defense." April 25, 1908.

"The Frenzy of Terror": The Church Panic of 1907

York Daily. "Architects Declare…Church Is Safe." November 23, 1907.

———. "Many Injured During…Panic." November 21, 1907.

———. "Was Quickel's Church About to Collapse?" November 22, 1907.

York Dispatch. "The Church Panic." November 21, 1907.

———. "Snyder Blamed for Hoover Murder." November 21, 1907.

York Gazette. "Lutheran Ministers Draw Moral Lessons." November 25, 1907.

"The Narrow Path": Last Call for "Peggy" Larue

Gazette and Daily. "Coroner's Jury to Hear Witnesses in Abbott Murder." August 13, 1924.

———. "Dorwart Enters Bail as Witness." August 14, 1924.

———. "Drink Crazed Youth Kills Woman." August 11, 1924.

———. "Drops Dead While Attending Court." January 6, 1925.

———. "Fred M'Lean…Held for October Court." September 11, 1924.

———. "Kid Mack Now in York County Jail." August 30, 1924.

———. "Material Witness Absent When Called." January 6, 1925.

———. "McLean Admission of Shooting Told on Witness Stand." January 8, 1925.

———. "McLean Arraigned Before Judge N. Sargeant Ross." October 29, 1924.
———. "M'Lean Found Guilty of Murder." January 10, 1925.
———. "M'Lean on Stand in His Own Defense." January 9, 1925.
———. "Murdered Woman…Identified by Her Relatives." August 12, 1924.
———. "Peggy Larue Lived a Dual Life." August 11, 1924.
———. "Postpone Hearing in Abbott Murder." August 15, 1924.
———. "Testimony Heard in Abbott Murder." August 28, 1924.

THE PERILS OF PARAMOURS

"Unsound Mind": Lost Loves of Johnny Coyle

Clay, Marianne. "County's Own Fatal Attraction." *York Daily Record*.
Laity, John. "Johnny Coyle Hanged for Killing His True Love." *Sunday News*, July 13, 1969.
Lehman, Garry. "Murder at Coyle's Ferry." Research paper.
MacPherson, B.P.M. "A Bit of History About Early Settlers." *Gettysburg Times*, columns published in 1962.
York Press. "Midnight Raid on the Grave of Coyle." May 2, 1884.

"One Sorrow After Another": The People v. Ervin Spangler

Gazette and Daily. "Another Murder Trial Underway." February 18, 1926.
———. "Mrs. Charles Meckley Shot by Lover." August 27, 1925.
———. "Mrs. Meckley Dies of Wounds." August 28, 1925.
———. "Much Progress in Spangler Murder." February 19, 1926.
———. "Sentence Passed by Judge Niles on Four Slayers." February 26, 1926.
———. "Spangler Say Woman Pulled Razor on Him." February 20, 1926.
———. "Two Accused Murderers Up at the Same Time." October 27, 1925.
———. "Verdict in Murder in Second Degree Against Spangler." February 22, 1926.
York Dispatch. "Murderer of Women Kills Self." December 17, 1932.

HELL HATH NO FURY

"Wickedest Creature": The Confession of Elizabeth Moore

"Confession of Elizabeth Moore." Transcript of Oyer and Terminer court proceeding, from the collection of the York County Heritage Trust.

"Blotting Out the Roses": The Winter of Kate Ness

Lloyd, June. "The Queen Of Jacobus: A Tragedy." *York Sunday News*, May 11, 2008.

Philadelphia North American. "Prison Bars Could Not Shut Out...Friends." February 28, 1903.

York Dispatch. "Catharine Ness Now Being Tried." January 10, 1902.

———. "Catharine Ness Salty Sentence." January 11, 1902.

———. "Kate Ness Is Sorry." October 30, 1901.

———. "Woman Attempts to Kill Her Lover." October 29, 1901.

York Gazette. "Bold Attempt at Murder." October 29, 1901.

———. "Catharine Ness Held." November 2, 1901.

———. "Kate Ness Convicted." January 12, 1902.

———. "Kate Ness Placed on Trial." January 10, 1902.

———. "More of the Ness Case." January 11, 1902.

"By Criminal Intimacy": The Black Widow Love Triangle

York Gazette. "Big Day for Prosecution in Brown Murder Trial." January 12, 1910.

———. "Brown's Brag and Big Gun Not Effective." June 24, 1909.

———. "Brown Guilty in Second Degree." January 14, 1910.

———. "Chemist Finds Strychnine in Tracey Stomach." June 30, 1909.

———. "Farm Hand's Death Looks Like Murder." June 15, 1909.

———. "First Degree Murder Verdict Against Brown." January 18, 1910.

———. "Important Day for Prosecution in Murder Case." October 22, 1909.

———. "Investigation of Poison Case Will Begin at Once." June 18, 1909.

———. "Josh Tracey Was a Victim of Foul Play." June 17, 1909.

———. "Jury in Brown Murder Case Tied Up Overnight." January 13, 1910.

———. "Minnie Tracey Poisoned Drink of Her Husband." June 22, 1909.

———. "More Murders May Yet Face Man and Woman." June 21, 1909.
———. "Mrs. Tracey and Brown Are Held for Court Without Bail." July 2, 1909.
———. "Mrs. Tracey and Brown Indicted by Grand Jury." August 24, 1909.
———. "Mrs. Tracey and William Brown Plead Not Guilty." August 25, 1909.
———. "Mrs. Tracey Anxious About Her Children." July 1, 1909.
———. "Mrs. Tracey Gets Off with Manslaughter Verdict." October 25, 1909.
———. "Neighbors Care for the Tracey Children." June 25, 1909.
———. "No Lawyer Secured for Tracey Defense." June 26, 1909.
———. "Other Admissions by Mrs. Tracey." June 29, 1909.
———. "Tracey Children on Stand Against Brown." January 11, 1910.
———. "Tracey Murder Case Comes Up Next Week." August 13, 1909.
———. "Verdict in Tracey Case a Miscarriage of Justice." October 26, 1909.
———. "Whitecappers After Brown Before Crime." June 23, 1909.
———. "William Brown Arrested." June 19, 1909.
———. "Witnesses Give Minute Account of Tracey Death." October 23, 1909.

Brutal Harvest

"Lunatic Fringe": The Hex Murder

Associated Press. "Blymyer Escaped From…Asylum During Ball Game." December 9, 1928.
———. "Decry Powwowing as Fraud Excuse." January 14, 1929.
———. "Evidence of Voodoo Quackery." December 5, 1928.
Butterfield, Roger. "The Witchcraft Murder." *Illustrated Detective Magazine*, April 1931.
Clarke, Caryl. "Infamous Home to Open." *York Daily Record*, June 5, 2007.
———. "Memories Tied to Murder." June 20, 2007.
———. "Puzzled by Hex Rejection." August 9, 2007.
Gazette and Daily. "Insanity Defense in Blymyer Trial." January 9, 1929.
———. "Jury Convicts Blymyer of First Degree Murder." January 10, 1929.
———. "Life Behind Bars Fate of Curry." January 12, 1929.
———. "Murder in Second Degree Is Verdict Passed Upon Hess." January 14, 1929.

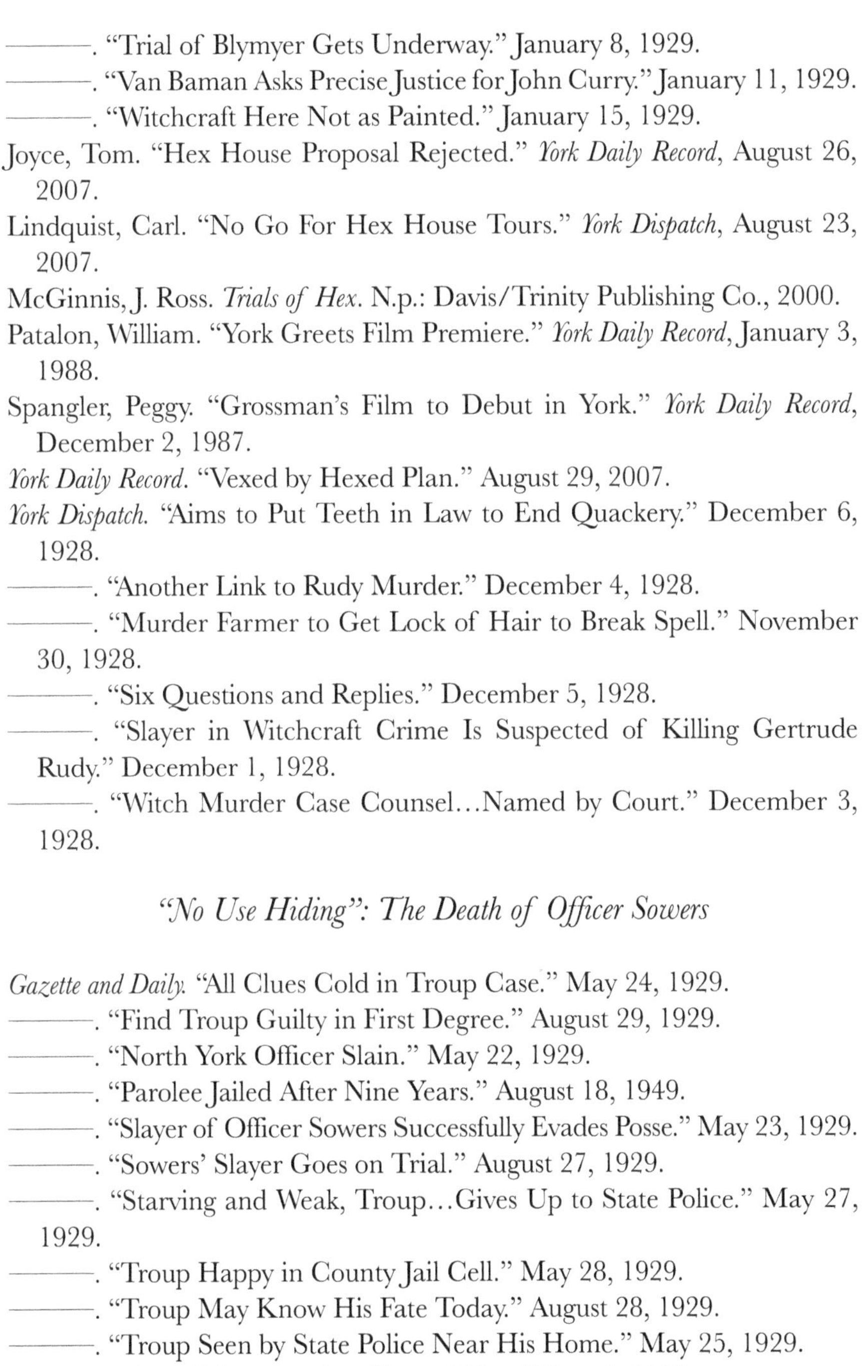

———. "Trial of Blymyer Gets Underway." January 8, 1929.

———. "Van Baman Asks Precise Justice for John Curry." January 11, 1929.

———. "Witchcraft Here Not as Painted." January 15, 1929.

Joyce, Tom. "Hex House Proposal Rejected." *York Daily Record*, August 26, 2007.

Lindquist, Carl. "No Go For Hex House Tours." *York Dispatch*, August 23, 2007.

McGinnis, J. Ross. *Trials of Hex*. N.p.: Davis/Trinity Publishing Co., 2000.

Patalon, William. "York Greets Film Premiere." *York Daily Record*, January 3, 1988.

Spangler, Peggy. "Grossman's Film to Debut in York." *York Daily Record*, December 2, 1987.

York Daily Record. "Vexed by Hexed Plan." August 29, 2007.

York Dispatch. "Aims to Put Teeth in Law to End Quackery." December 6, 1928.

———. "Another Link to Rudy Murder." December 4, 1928.

———. "Murder Farmer to Get Lock of Hair to Break Spell." November 30, 1928.

———. "Six Questions and Replies." December 5, 1928.

———. "Slayer in Witchcraft Crime Is Suspected of Killing Gertrude Rudy." December 1, 1928.

———. "Witch Murder Case Counsel…Named by Court." December 3, 1928.

"No Use Hiding": The Death of Officer Sowers

Gazette and Daily. "All Clues Cold in Troup Case." May 24, 1929.

———. "Find Troup Guilty in First Degree." August 29, 1929.

———. "North York Officer Slain." May 22, 1929.

———. "Parolee Jailed After Nine Years." August 18, 1949.

———. "Slayer of Officer Sowers Successfully Evades Posse." May 23, 1929.

———. "Sowers' Slayer Goes on Trial." August 27, 1929.

———. "Starving and Weak, Troup…Gives Up to State Police." May 27, 1929.

———. "Troup Happy in County Jail Cell." May 28, 1929.

———. "Troup May Know His Fate Today." August 28, 1929.

———. "Troup Seen by State Police Near His Home." May 25, 1929.

———. "Troup Threatened to Shoot Officer." June 1, 1929.

"Here Is a Warning": The Dietrich Family Tragedy

Gazette and Daily. "Dietrich Family Funeral Today." September 25, 1930.

———. "Farmer Near Spry Wipes Out His Entire Family with Axe." September 24, 1930.

York Dispatch. "Ax Slayer's Farm Sold." October 13, 1930.

———. "Farmer Turns His Home Into Shambles." September 24, 1930.

———. "5,000 Attend Sale on Dietrich Farm, Scene of Tragedy." October 11, 1930.

UNSOLVED

"Murder Hole": The Pigeon Hills Slaying

"Horrible Murder." Transcript of court proceedings from the collection of the York County Heritage Trust.

Snavely, Jim. "Pigeon Hills Still Guard Murder Secrets." *York Daily Record*, August 6, 1973.

York Gazette. "The Heidelberg Murder." December 17, 1878.

"Wrapped in Horror": A Crime Scene Sketch

History Society of York County. "Murder Victim's Art Displayed at Museum." July 3, 1959. Press release.

York Dispatch. "Heckert Arrest Stirs Officials." March 9, 1908.

York Gazette. "David Heckert Brutally Murdered in His Bed." February 16, 1908.

———. "David Heckert Not Killed by Blows." March 5, 1908.

———. "Finger Marks in Heckert Room Nearest Clue to Murderer." February 24, 1908.

———. "Heckert Arrest Has Added New Interest to the Murder Case." March 9, 1908.

———. "Heckert Slayer Did Not Enter House by Way of Ladder." February 29, 1908.

———. "John Heckert Arrested by Police for Carrying Gun." March 8, 1908.

———. "Murderer May Have Secured Much Gold." February 19, 1908.

———. "Murder Suspect Arrest May Be Made Within Day or Two." February 18, 1908.

———. "Saw Man in Rear of Heckert Home." February 17, 1908.

———. "$3,266.50 Is Found in the Heckert Home." February 23, 1908.

———. "Victim of Robbery at York Will Be Buried Today." February 18, 1908.

"This Darkest of Mysteries": The Murder of Gertrude Rudy

Gazette and Daily. "Girl Found Dead on Tracks." November 9, 1927.

———. "Man Who Told of Murder Jailed." April 12, 1928.

———. "Rudy Girl Murder Remains Mystery." April 5, 1928.

Hubley, Jim. "Other Old Murders Remain Unsolved." *York Daily Record*, July 8, 2000.

York Dispatch. "Another Link to Rudy Murder Chain." December 4, 1928.

———. "Slayer in Witchcraft Crime Is Suspected of Killing Gertrude Rudy." December 1, 1928.

ABOUT THE AUTHOR

Joseph David Cress is an award-winning journalist with twenty years of full-time newspaper experience. For twelve years, he has worked as a staff reporter with the *Sentinel* in Carlisle. *Murder & Mayhem in York County* is his third book with The History Press. Previous works include *Remembering Carlisle: Tales from the Cumberland Valley* and *Murder & Mayhem in Cumberland County*. Cress lives in York, Pennsylvania, with his wife, Stacey, dogs Dottie and Rosco and cats Chewie and Boone.

Courtesy of the Sentinel.

www.ingramcontent.com/pod-product-compliance
Lightning Source LLC
Chambersburg PA
CBHW060810100426
42813CB00004B/1021

9781540229854